Embracing a Loss
From Sorrow to Acceptance

A Journal Companionway

Kristen,

September 1991, you wrote words in my journal that I have treasured. It was a relief to know someone understood a mother's grief from miscarriage. I offer this copy of "Embracing..." as thanks for your wonderful comments and caring words. I hope this book finds you and your family well.

Best wishes,
Elisa
480-961-1783

I can also be reached at the address and web site on the back of this book or

Elisa Carrillo Baldry *at embaldry @hotmail.com*

Companionway Press, LLC
Tempe, Arizona

Warning Disclaimer

The design of this book is for the purpose of sharing like experiences. The information in this book is offered with the understanding that the author, publisher, and advisors are not rendering medical or professional services. This book is in no way a substitute for therapy, counseling, or medical advice. If you are currently in counseling or therapy, review the material with your therapist or physician. Application of any suggestion, treatment approach, or technique outlined in this book is the sole responsibility of the reader. The author and Companionway Press shall have neither liability nor responsibility to any person with respect to any loss or damage caused, or alleged to be caused, directly or indirectly by the information contained in this book.

Printed in the United States of America

Cover art by Tony Carrillo
Cover design by Enigma Design Graphics
Typesetting by Ross Typesetting

Dedication

To my children, who led me back to my
wellspring of discovery and profound love.

Acknowledgments

The making of this book has been a commitment dating back more than ten
years. It began with my own grief and loss from recurrent miscarriage, followed
by the loss of my sister. My world took on a form and hue I did not recognize.
Navigating through those bleak surroundings was something I had yet to learn.
Writing became my means of coping. Many encouraged me to share, and with
their encouragement, I offer this book as a navigational tool through the murky
surroundings of grief. I have many to thank for their care and encouragement:

To David, you were my life line. I thank God for you.

To Peter, who knew? We are still here together.

To Dr. Linnerson, you freed me in a way I never imagined possible when you
    asked me to share my writing. Thank you for your willingness to
    patiently lend an ear at a crucial time for me. Your time, talent,
    professionalism, and guidance were essential for my welfare and the
    welfare of my family. I am forever grateful.

To Teri Krull, for your wisdom and courageous willingness to walk with me and
    "shine some light" into the dark caverns I needed to explore.

To Linda Brost, your kindness is unforgettable.

To Suzanne Helzer, for your honesty and ideas. You keep me thinking.

To Leslie Delp, for letting me know my writing touched someone in a positive
    way. Your call re-established my commitment to share.

To Rachel Faldet and Karen Fitton, for bringing grieving parents together to
    share words of healing. Special thanks to Rachel Faldet for offering your
    comments and encouraging me to complete this project.

To Dr. Roden, for your kindness and willingness to guide me through the
    process of publishing.

To Miss Morgan and Ness Marie, your momma loves you.

Preface

Everyday throughout this country thousands of women suffer the loss of a baby through the events of a miscarriage. National statistics show that fifteen percent of all conceptions end up aborting. In fact, this is such a common event that each of us are unknowingly coming into daily contact with someone who is suffering pain and mourning the loss of a child that will never be seen or held. Historically, this mental anguish has been privately endured as a woman struggles with the many questions of why, when, and what now. Also historically, medical professionals were ill-equipped and unprepared to deal with the psychological damage done when bereavement is left unattended. That is no longer the case as research and counselors have now recognized the large number of individuals that have unworked and unresolved grief over the loss of a pregnancy. Over the past ten years, many support groups with supportive literature have cropped up and have made a distinctive difference in the lives of those bereaved by a loss. However, this type of group support requires willingness for the bereaved to publicly open themselves to wounds that are sometimes very private, personal issues, best held close to a woman's heart. It is out of this need for private reflection, and the recognition that bereaved women need a personal resource to help them heal that Elisa Baldry has provided us with a personal journal from grief to resolve.

I first met Elisa and Peter years ago when I delivered their first child. Early on it was very evident, the passion that they had to become parents. This was only matched by the intense grief they experienced as they lost pregnancy after pregnancy. As a physician, I realized that it was not only my responsibility to explain why, and investigate causes, but also to help Elisa and Pete keep their passion to become parents. These were not easy times as we struggled through doubt, depression, miscommunication, and fear, but never did Elisa lose her spirit or passion. I watched as she fought through her feelings while she desperately searched for a reason for her losses, but more importantly, a solution that would bring her a child that she could hold and love. I often wondered what held her together, but privately knew that Peter, God, and her God-given spirit to be a mother kept her passion stronger than her grief and fear. Finally through the heartache and tears, and the miracles of modern medicine, Elisa and Peter became parents again. Today, Elisa is living her dream while she and Peter nurture their three children in Chandler, Arizona.

Early in our journey when Elisa had lost three pregnancies, I often told her that God would someday show her the reason for her losses. Elisa's journal is a tribute and testament to those lost and unseen children, for it is through their loss and her journey that we have been given such a valuable resource. Elisa, as your children surely rest in God's arms, may you and Peter find comfort in the fact that the purpose of their loss was to benefit our gain as we receive perspective and healing from reading *Embracing a Loss From Sorrow to Acceptance.* May God bless this work and all those who encounter its healing balm.

Steven M. Linnerson, M.D., F.A.C.O.G.

Contents

Foreword

I first met Elisa in July of 1990 when she was referred to me for counseling after a miscarriage. She was hurt and angry with the medical field for their inability to compassionately deal with her loss. She felt misunderstood by friends and family. And while Elisa's experience was unique, it was not dissimilar to other cases in my practice. What separated Elisa from other clients who had experienced loss was her approach in dealing with grief.

Within the first months of treatment, Elisa shared her journal with me. In it she explored her emotions and expressed her dreams with candor. She wrote as only one who has experienced grief and loss could. Beyond my newfound appreciation of Elisa's talent as a writer, I quickly came to value her abilities as a teacher. In sharing her stories she not only was a mother, sister, wife, friend and teacher, she was all of us.

Elisa's treatment with me ended in early 1992. She continued to write in her journal, and it was months later that she offered it as a tool for use in my treatment of clients who had also experienced loss. I gratefully accepted her offer and found the journal to be a valuable therapy resource. My clients enthusiastically reported they felt not only understood by Elisa, but also helped by her shared experiences.

You are now presented with that same opportunity. *Embracing a loss From Sorrow to Acceptance* is an eloquent, moving account of one person's journey of loss. Not only will you hear Elisa's stories, you will be encouraged to share your experiences, your own stories. Through your own discovery, you too can "embrace loss" and take your journey "from sorrow to acceptance." Elisa's "introspection, growth and healing" is not only inspiring but also a gift to the reader. Move forward with confidence. Someone understands. Someone is listening. I thank Elisa for her courageous gift of personal experience and understanding.

Teri V. Krull, CISW, LLC
Board Certified Diplomate
Registered Play Therapy Supervisor
Director, Center for Positive Regard

Author's Note: Proffered Hand

I have experienced the grief of loss a number of times in my life. I have said farewell to family and friends. The most profound were the losses of my babies through miscarriage and the loss of my eldest sister from suicide. Following the initial shock and numbness came the heart wrenching pain of loss. My life is changed and forever will be. Acceptance of that change was difficult at best. Their passing necessitated introspection, growth and healing. The grief following the loss of my sister was understood and recognized by others. The lives of my babies were brief, their presence never reaching beyond my body and my heart where the loss of them weighed so heavily. Before I could openly grieve the loss of my babies, it was necessary to dispel the myth that losing a baby due to miscarriage is basically an insignificant occurrence that has little or no effect on the emotional or physical state of the woman or her partner.

I realized how fragile the balance of happiness and stability are in this existence. I remember the deep sadness when I felt I could no longer live my own life. I do not feel immune to being in that place again. Looking back, I see a need for a purposeful avenue to accompany one to the depths while providing a tool to work through the ordeal.

The concept of a journal within a journal originated from the realization that although some aspects of grief appear to be universal, there is a uniqueness to each experience that deserves to be expressed. As a vehicle of self-expression, here is an outlet for defining the personal facets of the grief experience. There is a need for sharing and remembering and so I invite you to participate through writing, to personalize this journal and use it as a tool for exploring and healing. I hope this journal will become a companion and later a cherished remembrance of one, whose presence and loss were deeply felt.

In the midst of the devastation due to your loss, it is my wish to offer this collection of writings. It symbolically represents my offering a hand to touch you and remain with you throughout your sorrow.

Elisa Baldry

Journal Entry: Why Write?

Have you ever spoken and had no one willing to listen? I have. Some looked right at me and when I began to talk, they turned away. It was as though I were speaking a foreign language that no one understood or was interested in learning. They didn't take the time to tell me they were not interested but at least they didn't insult me by pretending to listen when it was clear they had no interest in the topic I wanted to discuss. The experience made me feel like I was in my own space and time, apart from the rhythm of my surroundings. Motion occurred at a different pace so that everything passed, silent and unaffected by the issues that moved me.

I have a similar perception of grief. Being shrouded in grief was an isolating experience for me. Everyday events seemed out of place and without meaning. All focus moved inward when the numbness disappeared, and the burning ache consumed my insides. It seemed like a natural reaction to pull inward when I was in pain until I discovered that is the place where the pain was most intense.

Grief is a difficult subject to address; people may feel uncomfortable with the accompanying emotions. For some it is a painful reminder of past experiences or an unwelcome reminder of the inevitable some people fear. Loss is inevitable, unfortunately what is not inevitable is that the bereaved person will continue to welcome life's experiences. In the depths of grief I found myself asking: How do I cope? How do I continue? Where will I find the strength? I was told to write and although at the time I saw no benefit in doing so, I took up my pen for lack of a better way to proceed. I received wise counsel. Writing was a necessary part of grieving for me. Through the written word my pain, my thoughts, and my emotions were clearly expressed, allowing others to examine and relate to me in ways my spoken words could not convey. Attempting to understand and cope with the flood of emotions that gripped me so painfully, I experienced through writing a better understanding of my personal journey through life and death. I have learned about grief and its many painful avenues. In exploring the depths of my sorrow, I discovered this tangible means of expressing emotion had become a companion throughout. My journal held my thoughts when I needed time away. It kept memories I now hold dear, giving permanence to those I lost.

I question the belief that forgetting and getting on with life is an adequate approach to coping with grief. Those who examine their grief experience can potentially move ahead confidently, having gained personal insight and strength. Self-expression and exploration are necessary, but where do you turn if you do not wish to "burden others with your problems?" The written word is a powerful tool. Writing allows you to address issues when you need to be address them rather than when someone, "can relate" or is willing to listen. Writing can enhance communication by allowing the individual to organize thoughts and expand on ideas. At times it may seem as though you are speaking a foreign language. Thoughts and emotions become closely tied when grief engulfs us. It is difficult to describe emotions with words but I encourage you to persist. Journaling provides a means of revealing the very personal thoughts that can offer enlightenment and inspiration. Everyone possesses a wellspring of inspiration deep inside that should not go unexplored. Learn to tap that inner resource, it can be a tremendous source of strength.

Journal Prompt: Unclaimed Treasures

Dear Reader,
Journaling is the process of recording thoughts and observations. Relaxing your mind and focusing on the details of what you are observing helps to free your pen. Writing is enhanced by description, even subtle descriptions expand the view of a subject to broaden understanding. Examine the big events in your life but do not overlook the tidbits. Stop to examine them closely, record what you see, learn from them. Your journal may become the treasure-trove that holds all the enriching thoughts and memories that have shaped you and that you may come to value.

This exercise is designed to encourage your mind to open up and allow your thoughts to flow. Use your imagination to fill in the blanks to complete the story. Your responses may consist of a single word or several words if you choose.

Unclaimed Treasures

I awoke from my sleep early one morning. I knew it was early because I noticed _____. Looking around my room I saw _____.
Sleep eluded me and so I decided to go for a walk. I opened the door and felt _____ as I stepped out on the _____. The _____ felt _____ against my face. I smelled the scent of _____ in the air. It reminded me of _____. I headed in a direction opposite my usual path and happened along a road new to me. As I proceeded to follow its direction, I stumbled on a _____ in my path. While I managed to keep myself from falling, my eye was drawn to a small worn _____ lying in the dirt along the roadside. The thought occurred to me that I miss the practice of walking the beaten path in search of those things that have fallen along the way. As a child I never missed the opportunity to search for unclaimed treasures: an unusual bottle cap, a colorful rock, a ball-point pen that still had ink. I decided then to again adopt the practice of searching for and collecting valuable tidbits discarded. My search would begin today. The excitement at the thought of creating a new treasure-trove was invigorating. I continued down the path with a purpose. New discoveries were awaiting me.

If a thought comes to mind that interests you or serves as a reminder of something you would like to explore further, continue with your thoughts in writing. Do not concern yourself with spelling or how to punctuate a sentence, your thoughts and ideas are of most value.

Journal Entry: Painful Embrace

I had a conversation with a friend the other day. She described a personal experience to me that caused her pain. She had experienced a miscarriage. She followed with a description of another woman's extremely painful experience. My friend seemed to be making an attempt to put her own experience into perspective. Apologetically, she explained why she should not hurt or grieve as much as this other woman. She perceived the other woman's experience to be the more painful. Consequently my friend reasoned, expressing her own pain or grief was unacceptable.

This idea of tucking pain away or hiding the need to grieve seems to be accepted and even admired as a show of strength. The flaw in this logic is that someone else's pain will not erase our own. One can consider someone else's pain and reason that their own situation is not so bad. The reasoning may lend encouragement and motivation to work through personal pain to overcome a difficult situation. One must realize, first, we share the ability to feel pain, not the reasons something is or is not painful. Second, the recipient does not control pain's degree. Anyone who has ever braced themselves and still been floored by a painful outcome knows what this statement means.

One may accept pain and even celebrate it as a realistic part of life but unless we acknowledge the pain we feel and experience it honestly, the pain and grief can re-emerge and have their influence another day. It is essential to avoid tucking away the resulting emotions. Constructive personal expression through journaling can allow the individual some influence over emotion. If you feel pain, express it in some honest way. The admission is a part of the healing process. Like air to the wound, it can allow the wound to breathe and prevent the festering infection of neglect.

Part I

The Grief of Miscarriage

Dear Reader,

The poem, "Flowing Red," depicts the physical event of miscarriage and a mother's agonizing grief for her child. The grief of a mother for her child is often overlooked in the event of miscarriage.

Journal Entry: Flowing Red

Grief filled, gripped by sorrow,
Mighty fist clenched unforgivingly around her heart.
Seeping through trembling white knuckles, a warm red river flows;
Miscarried life retreats in wine colored drops.
Unwilling heart fights to be freed,
Mindful of briefly held dreams left unopened.
Deeply wounded, feeling betrayed,
She pleads for the ebb of the relentless thrusts.
She lays spent wondering why she has been miscast.
Limp and weakened she bleeds,
Like red grapes squeezed until sun sweetened nectar flows
Filling the casks with their wine.
Clenched teeth bear down,
Releasing the taste of bitter red wine on her tongue.
Unwilling host painfully contracts, rhythmically relinquishing its prize.

E.B.

Dear Reader,

The grief of miscarriage is a complex grief. A vagueness surrounds miscarriage, especially an early loss. Should I grieve for someone I knew for such a short time? Do I have that right? Do I have a need to express grief?

Having a son, the experience of being a mother was not new to me. Regardless of the stage of development my baby had reached, I knew what I had lost through miscarriage. I had lost a baby, not tissue, not a group of cells, my baby.

Journal Entry: Mother's Day

I am one of the fortunate ones. I have a son to hold and as my doctor says, "someone to celebrate the holidays with." My son's name is David. My pregnancy with him was ideal. I experienced the innocent bliss of pregnancy, excitedly tracking his growth through pictures in books every several weeks. Lennert Nilsson's, *A Child Is Born,* was my favorite book.

My own growth and expansion amazed me. How was this huge belly ever going to fit discreetly onto my frame again? I pictured my belly after delivery like a stretched and deflated balloon, complete with wrinkles from over stress, heavily sagging to my thighs underneath my clothing. Even if I could wad up the excess, where would I hide it? Eventually to my relief, my body repaired itself, amazingly shrinking to leave only some puckers and a few faint lines like overly stretched seams. The delivery was typical with no complications and I was overwhelmed by the joy of holding a strong healthy son.

Today however is Mother's Day, a bittersweet holiday like David's birthday, Christmas, and our wedding anniversary. When I had David, I felt like I had fallen into a dream that made me happier than I had ever been before. Just as I started to relax with the realization that my dream might finally be coming true, I woke up. On David's birthday, our family gets together to celebrate. It is always nice, but when everyone leaves and evening comes, I find myself crying because we were supposed to be celebrating the birth of our second baby too. My due date was August sixth, the day after David's birthday but we lost our baby in January. I have always loved the Christmas holidays, so when my doctor told me I was going to have a Christmas baby; I was very happy. That year at the end of May, we did not celebrate our ninth wedding anniversary because I was in bed bleeding. I realized then that our Christmas baby was gone too. Now the Christmas holidays bring mixed feelings. It is impossible to keep the wave of sadness from surfacing. My chances of having more children I am told, are slim.

I look at David and I am amazed at how quickly he has grown. I love watching him change. It is exciting when he learns something new but he is growing up so fast! I remember him as a tiny baby. I remember the warm feeling when I held him. I remember rocking him and playing with his tiny fingers and toes but I feel like I blinked and those times were gone. I was hoping to have four children. I wanted to watch them grow up together. It seems like such a luxury that some women are able to hold their tiny baby and still enjoy watching their other children growing, each one at a different stage. Sometimes I wish I didn't want my family so badly. I put all my eggs into one basket by allowing my dream of a house full of children to be the one thing I wanted more than anything else. I know I should count my blessings and be thankful for the opportunity to watch David grow, but every time someone mentions how big David is and how quickly he has grown; the feeling is again bittersweet. I am proud of him, but I wish I could make time stand still so I could hold on to him a little longer.

On my worst days I look at my son and thank God for him again. But while I am looking at him, I am still feeling the pain of the two babies I lost. They were also gifts from God and I treasure them too. I can't sleep. I can't stop asking for answers to questions that no one seems able to provide for me. I can't stop hurting. The pain is hard to describe, it is deep inside me and it won't lessen its grip on me. I have tried to make the pain go away. I tried running from it by denying it was even there. I knew the pain was there but I was afraid of how it would affect me if I acknowledged it. I didn't want the pain to overtake me, but it did. There is no escaping the pain, it is very real and can't be denied or ignored. I thought I would finally feel some relief or at least be able to live with the pain when I found out I was pregnant again. I was happy again but the happiness was short-lived, just like the pregnancy before it had been. We wanted our babies. We planned, we prepared, we waited, and finally they came. We were so excited. Who could have known we would never be able to see them or hold them? Who could have known they would come to us and then leave us so suddenly? It amazes me how deeply I felt their presence. In a very short time they found a place in my heart. In my heart and in my dreams my two babies will remain very real. They will be loved and will always be missed.

There is a longing that accompanies the pain when you lose a baby you have only been able to carry for a short time. I long to have held them and rocked them, even if it were only long enough to have been able to say good-bye.

E.B.

Journal Prompt: Memories

Write about the loss you are grieving. Record your experience. If you need help getting started, consider the following suggestions.

If you are grieving the loss of your baby, you might remember:
the anticipation during pregnancy
plans you made in preparation for your baby
you may be able to describe how you felt following the loss
of your baby
if so, record thoughts that crossed your mind before or
after your loss
record a memory of an event that occurred before or
following your loss

Dear Reader,

From a medical standpoint miscarriage is fairly straightforward. It is a natural process that in most cases requires little or no help from a doctor. In the majority of cases, a woman can have a successful pregnancy following a miscarriage. The human body is an amazing machine. But this amazing machine holds life, making me a mother. When the amazing machine does not succeed in sustaining life, I am a mother who grieves. During pregnancy, I experience love for my baby. Following a miscarriage, I experience the pain of loss and an intense longing for my unborn child.

Journal Entry: Clinically Speaking Versus Mother's View

When I was experiencing my first miscarriage, I was told I had a "false pregnancy." I looked up the term in a medical dictionary. It said that it is not an uncommon mistake for an elderly, childless woman to delude herself with the hope that she is about to bear a child when the abdomen is enlarging simply due to the increasing development of fat. This condition is known as pseudocyesis or false pregnancy. I have never understood why that term was used to describe the pregnancy I lost. I had a positive pregnancy test. I was even given a due date and I am not yet old or fat.

That conversation with my doctor was unforgettable. Slowly and distinctly, as if for emphasis, that portion of our conversation played itself over and over in my mind. The emotions continued to hit me hard with each repetition. I realized there was some aspect of his explanation that demanded my attention. In time I learned through personal exploration, the origin of my grief. As a mother grieving the loss of her baby, I could not allow the clinical view to go unchallenged. I believe that when conception occurs, there is a human life. I could not accept the term "false pregnancy" because it did not recognize or respect the life that was lost. I was told there was "nothing there," only cells that failed to continue. That was my baby! Unfortunately, that may have been as far as it had come in its development, but that was my baby. In my heart my baby was very real and is still. It hurt to lose it, no matter how short its existence.

I cup my treasures in my hands and when I open them to look inside, I still see gold while other people just see dust. I don't understand why people who can respect the value of a life being sustained during pregnancy, find it so difficult to respect the loss of that life...a life that is conceived but ends before birth becomes null and void in the eyes and hearts of some. I still value the lives

I miscarried; my heart still remembers their presence and aches because they are gone.

I read an article on miscarriage in *Parenting*, that said, "After one miscarriage the chances of subsequent live birth are almost 87 percent and even after two miscarriages, a woman has a 60 percent chance of carrying the next baby to term. It's only after three losses in a row that the odds drop to 40 percent."

When you find out you are pregnant, all you have to do is get from point A to point B. It is very straightforward; you just have to jump over the pit. What pit? It is really nothing to worry about, chances are slim that you will actually fall in. I tried to jump over the pit. The opening was small but I fell in. People do not always realize how difficult it can be to climb out of that pit. It can seem small and insignificant to those standing on the outside looking in. On the inside, it is dark and lonely. I became very disoriented, and I was so afraid. I climbed out of the pit. I still carry some scars and bruises, but I made it out. The next time I tried, I fell in again. I want to get from point A to point B so badly, I'm ready to try even now. What I need to know, is how I'm supposed to get over that pit if the opening just keeps getting wider.

E.B.

Journal Prompt: Concerns

There may be aspects of your experiences that have left you confused, afraid or in some way unsettled. You may find that describing those aspects of your experiences in writing will free your mind and allow you to better address your concerns.

Are there concerns that remain? List those that come to mind. Follow-up with a detailed description of each concern.

Journal Prompt: Information Gathering

Gathering information may help you to address areas of concern. A mother once told me that gathering information about her situation helped her to better understand her doctor's explanations and gave her confidence when she needed to make decisions.

Brainstorm and list possible sources available for information that may answer your questions or further clarify your situation. For example, the Internet, pamphlets from the doctor's office, books, magazines, local support groups, etc.

Journal Entry: Constructive Confrontation

The frustrating thing about miscarriage is that it usually leaves so few clues as to its cause that most questions remain unanswered. In the beginning, I was left in the dark. I didn't know why I had miscarried. Eventually, the more common causes were ruled out. If I had three unexplained miscarriages, it was likely I could have more. The possibility of never being able to carry another baby to term was also real. I continued to wonder if I had caused my miscarriages in spite of the reassurance from my doctor that I had not. If he did not know the cause, how could he really know it was not my fault? The feeling of helplessness came from wondering what else I could do. I was so careful when I became pregnant. I changed my diet before we even tried to conceive. I exercised but was careful to avoid anything strenuous once I became pregnant. I tried to relax and put my feet up when I could. I was criticized for wanting to be so careful but I needed to know I was taking care of my baby the only way I knew how. I am glad I did because it turned out to be the only form of mothering I was able to give them. We never knew just how far my pregnancies had progressed. What was seen in an ultrasound never correlated with the number of weeks that had passed since my pregnancy test. Due to an auto-immune disorder, my body did not properly recognize and protect the baby. My immune system attacked the baby's developing tissue as it would any foreign invader, leaving little to see in an ultrasound but a normally developing sack.

After I had my miscarriages, people were anxious to tell me the stories of all those they knew, who in their minds had more painful experiences than mine. My need to talk to them was not to compare my own experience with someone else's, in order to say I had it worse than anyone else. I was trying to find someone who could help me understand the pain I was feeling and help me deal with it. Instead, I was told not to feel badly because there was no fetus for me to see. I understood their thinking. There is no doubt in my mind that a late miscarriage or stillbirth is an extremely painful experience, but it is impossible to compare one person's reaction and experience with another and then fairly judge who has the right to feel worse. Who has the right to make that kind of judgment and what is the benefit of doing so? One person can experience a divorce and hurt inside, while someone else may be relieved to be free from the ties of the relationship. I can only speculate as to why two people who seem to have had similar experiences react so differently. I do not think anyone would argue against the fact that a divorce can be a devastating and painful experience, but it seems to me that everyone has a right to express individual feelings. Just as one woman may be thrilled to find out she is pregnant, another may be devastated by the same news. I know someone who was relieved when she miscarried. She is at a point in her life where she is working to achieve goals that are important to her. She is not prepared right now to make the commitment required to raise a child. Our reactions to miscarriage were very different. Even those who may have wanted to be pregnant and were looking forward to being parents may not react in the same way, but each one is entitled to have their feelings respected. To make light of anyone's situation or tell them they are wrong to grieve, is insensitive and only adds to the hurt and feeling of aloneness. I had had all I could take of people telling me in one way or another that I was wrong to feel the way I did about the loss of my babies. **"After all,"** they said, **"you only had miscarriages."** I tried desperately to make them see as I did, the value and significance of the lives that were once there. Not only did they not understand my grief but many of them no longer wanted to be around me. I felt isolated in my grief and resented those who I thought were close to me when they turned away.

I struggled to overcome the pain that comes from losing someone whose life is important to me. I struggled to learn why those who knew me did not understand my perspective and seemed instead to offer comments, often impatiently, that contradicted my own. In response, I wrote. I wrote all I wanted to express but was not given the opportunity to say. I chose my words carefully, expressing heart and soul on paper. I captured every painful thought and held it fast while I confronted it, challenging ideas and beliefs contrary to my own. It was my defense for combating the intense emotions that threatened to consume me. The process of recording a response to the comments that most frustrated me allowed me to eventually put them from my mind, satisfied that I had spoken out against them.

The following are the comments I had a need to respond to:

During my first miscarriage I was examined after the bleeding had started, I was told I didn't have to stop working. Just before my surgery, I was told I would be fine tomorrow, "business as usual tomorrow." *Did they really think my baby's life was so insignificant that I could continue with my daily routine and pretend nothing had happened? The comments people made and their reactions toward my situation suggested I should be able to put the experience aside after a short time and live my life just as before.* **"We knew you had your surgery on Tuesday, so we figured you would be over it by now."** *The pain experienced and the healing that must take place are not due to a physical condition. The pain I feel goes much deeper and is more agonizing than any physical pain I have ever experienced. After two years, the healing is nowhere near completion.*

"Your miscarriage was nature's way and probably for the best. Besides, you have a beautiful little boy at home." *My miscarriages were nature's way of dealing with a pregnancy my body could no longer sustain. But this explanation is used too often to explain a miscarriage. What is overlooked*

17

is a condition that needs to be addressed because in some cases the condition can be avoided a second or third time. I do have a beautiful little boy at home, but the children I lost are also precious to me and I grieve for them still.

"My mom had a miscarriage and she said it's no big deal." *With every baby I lost, I lost a part of myself. I know my experience and feelings are difficult for some to relate to or understand. I only ask that you try to understand and respect the depth of my feelings.*

"Oh, just try not to think about it." *I needed my friend to listen. It was impossible not to think about what had happened and what I had lost.*

"At least it was early and there was nothing to see." *Not only was my baby gone but because there was nothing to see, any chance to learn why my pregnancy had failed or to find out if it was a condition that could be prevented next time, was also gone. I was left with no baby and no answers.*

"You were lucky, you only had a false pregnancy. My friend lost a baby after five months, imagine how she must feel." *As it turned out, I did not have a "false pregnancy." My doctor said later he should not have used that term. The cause of my miscarriages was eventually attributed to an auto-immune disorder. I did not feel the least bit lucky. I was expecting a baby. I wanted my baby, just as I am sure her friend wanted hers. To have my baby taken from me with no explanation was very painful. The time I carried my baby made no difference; two years later I am still experiencing the pain of that loss. My heart and prayers go out to her friend because of the pain and frustration she and her family must endure.*

"At least you know you can get pregnant." *This comment was made by a friend who had been trying to get pregnant but had not yet conceived. It was made shortly after my second miscarriage. My question to her was, "What good does it do to be able to get pregnant if you can no longer carry a pregnancy to term?" There is no comfort in knowing you can conceive without the hope of ever seeing or holding your baby.*

"Oh Lisa! Women who have stillbirths have it a lot worse than you." *I do not pretend to know how those women feel. The ones I know who have experienced the pain of a stillbirth treasure the pictures and the lock of hair they keep in memory of their child. They are not the ones who tell me I should be able to put aside the pain and frustration because they know how difficult it is to accept having their baby taken from them. I can not describe the longing and helplessness that accompanies the loss of a baby. I find myself struggling to endure it.*

"You're depressed? Well welcome to the world of PMS. It's just hormones. It happens to me all the time." *The person who made this comment has never been diagnosed with PMS. I do not believe she understands the struggle undertaken by women who must truly live with the effects of PMS, any* *more than she understands the pain, the longing, and the frustration experienced by those who have lost children and continue their attempts to bring their children into this world, only to be disappointed.*

"You just have to be strong." *What is not recognized is that it takes tremendous strength just to get through each day.*

"You know, you really need to change your attitude. You really lack faith. Why do you worry about things you can't control?" *God alone is in the position to judge the depth of my faith. My attitude will not change as long as I grieve for the children I have lost. I worry about things I cannot control when something as precious to me as my children are being taken away. I want to know why. I want to fix whatever is wrong so when I become pregnant I will eventually have a baby to hold and love and watch grow. My family is too important to me to be able to dismiss what is happening. I will continue to ask questions and search for a way to keep my babies alive. I will do whatever I can to realize my dream of a family.*

"I know just how you feel. My sister-in-law has been trying to have a baby for five years." *Before I had a miscarriage, I imagined the experience would be painful but I was not prepared for the intensity of emotions that can follow the experience. I do not pretend to understand how other people are feeling when they must endure a difficult situation. Instead, I try to respect the difficulty of their situation and offer support when I can. I have learned that the extent of the emotional strain cannot be fully understood by standing on the outside looking in.*

"We know you're not going to the baby shower because you're jealous that she's having a baby and you're not, but we think you should be able to put that aside for her sake. Imagine how she's going to feel if you're not there." *Baby showers can be a wonderful way to celebrate the coming of a new baby. It is fun to get caught up in the excitement by planning and preparing for the arrival of each new baby. I used to get caught up in the excitement; I planned baby showers for five friends. But I must ask my friends to try to understand that while my excitement for them is still there, what goes through my mind when I sit and look at all the little clothes and toys is very different from before. They are now reminders of painful experiences I am struggling to live with, just as I struggle with the daily reminders that bring the depression back so suddenly. If you notice I am not there, please remember that my thoughts and prayers are with you. But try to understand that I am in the middle of a struggle that I hope you will never experience but at times is so overwhelming that I think it will beat me. Please allow me the space I need without passing judgment on me.*

When I listen to the comments about miscarriage that imply it is just a painless and necessary function of nature, I realize those who see it that way are only looking at the surface. I see life and experience joy at its beginning and experience pain from the realization of its end. My comfort comes from knowing that life in its many forms is an extension of God that is both treasured and protected. It comes to us from Him and returns to Him at its end. I do not have to justify to anyone what I have lost or justify the pain I feel. I know and God knows the reasons for both. He listens and does not try to stifle me. Instead, in spite of all the hurt, He helps me continue to grow.

E.B.

Journal Prompt: Some Well-Intentioned Comments Hurt

Some well-intentioned comments hurt. Writing a response allows you to examine the hurt and better understand personal feelings. Addressing hurtful comments eases anger and resentment. Organizing thoughts to enhance communication enables you to confidently and effectively respond to similar comments in the future.

Write a response to any hurtful comments, even those made with the best of intentions...

Journal Prompt: Time Away

Time away from difficult situations may be necessary. It is not a show of cowardice but gentle tending to a healing heart. Everyday occurrences and special occasions may evoke thoughts and memories resulting in a flood of emotions difficult to control. Situations that were once enjoyable can be emotionally challenging and sometimes threatening.

Are there situations that you find difficult? Consider the reasons why these situations may be challenging.

These situations are difficult for me because...

If you have listed an event that you believe will be emotionally overwhelming, you may consider an alternative to attending, such as: sending flowers, sending a gift, writing a letter, sending a card, etc...

Think about how you might respond.

In response I will...

Part II

Exploring and Coping
With the Emotions of Grief

Dear Reader,

I have been told that the grief of miscarriage is not the same as the grief following the loss of a loved one but it was for me. This entry was written following the loss of my sister. The grief from losing her may be easier to understand than the grief of miscarriage, however the similarities are worth noting: the sense of loss, the pain, the frustration, the feelings of helplessness, even the unanswered questions of why, were there. There was no difference. The grief was a result of losing a life that continues to be important to me.

My experiences with miscarriage and the loss of my sister were devastating, and yet I wouldn't ask that they not be my own because that would mean giving up the privilege of being touched by those lives. Each union was a privilege I will never regret, however painful the loss.

Journal Entry: Sister

The house is dim and quiet. I am awake and alone. I am awake because I sleep at the wrong times. I sleep when I am tired and awake when I am angry. I should try to reverse that, perhaps then I could act out my anger in dreams and arise rested and healed. I wonder where the dreams would take me...to fields, dark and damp, where I could confront demons face to face and not have to guess their disguise?

At one time I mistook anger for one of the demons until I learned to wield its power. Anger directed inward withers the tenderest of emotions, the tendrils that allow individuality to thrive. Some people become numb and hollow; others ache and burn inside like a wound festering, poisoned. Turned and manipulated, anger becomes a driving force that overcomes fear and propels me to another place.

But where are the demons?

My feet are firmly planted in the earth. In the darkness, I smell the cool dampness enveloping me. My fear has dissipated into the surrounding mist. My anger is my sword and my shield.

Where are the demons?

I want to hit them hard and lay them low. I want them to know the strength of my anger. I want them to know I have lost the paralyzing fear. The sounds of stillness are all I hear.

Where are the demons?

Instead, I see the image of you whom I love. I want to hear your voice, your laughter, feel the warmth of you near. I call out often. Why did you go? Were you hurting? I don't want to believe that you were.

There are memories...two little girls sharing stories because I couldn't read and you said the stories were too good to miss: Tom Sawyer, Charlotte's Web. Remember our hikes to the cross on the mountain...so calm and beautiful up there? Racing to the bottom of the mountain, trying to avoid the cactus, it added to the thrill of the race! Poor Lois, prickles everywhere.

Remember when we rebuilt the carburetor in your truck? We hadn't repaired anything since our tricycles. Fixing our "trikes" involved turning them upside down, spinning the tires and removing pebbles stuck in the tread. Spraying water on our tricycles and letting them drip dry always fixed them right up. "A carburetor is different," I said. "What if we can't do it?" I said. "Eighty percent confidence, twenty percent know-how," you said, "besides we have a book."

You suggested I remember the first half of the parts we removed. You would remember the second half. That worked great, until I forgot my half! I had not seen anything so confusing since Dr. Seuss' Throm-dim-bu-lator fell apart. Did that skrux or that snux fit into the snoor? You figured it out, although I don't know how.

Remember my wedding and the bug that flew out of your flowers and landed on the end of your nose? Remember the night I had to go to the hospital? It was a relief to hear your voice over the phone. It was midnight but you would be right over. I didn't feel like crying until you walked through the door. I said, "I'm scared." You said, "I love you."

Remember the basket of flowers you sent to me on the first of May? You remembered how I loved making baskets out of notebook paper and hanging them on our neighbors' doorknobs when I was a kid...notebook paper baskets stuffed with bluebells and dandelions. I still have the card you sent. It has yellowed with age but it says, "Sister, for all the things you figured out in childhood...Happy May Day!" signed, "Goc." The card has a little girl holding a bunch of green, yellow, and blue balloons. The bright red one is floating away; that one makes me think of you.

For all I may have figured out, I still have not learned how to miss you without hurting and being angry that you took yourself away. I don't feel anger toward you but toward whatever demons chased you away. I couldn't think about you and me for a long, long time. It hurt too much. I am not afraid anymore. The anger, I have controlled.

Where are the demons? Why did you go?

E.B.

Journal Prompt: Acknowledging a Loss

"There are times I feel sad, and the emptiness seems unbearable. There are times the hurt seems to be smothering me."

Acknowledging a loss or disappointment and what it personally means can help in deciphering the origin of the pain.

To begin writing, I will often capture a passing thought on paper, like the one above. I will then expand on that thought by both questioning the emotions and explaining their origin when I can. Or, I may continue with a description of emotions without any other input. The acknowledgment of the depth of emotion gives me rest until a time when I may be ready to take a closer look.

You may be able to describe a similar experience and explore the accompanying thoughts and emotions. The reasons for the emotions are exclusively your own, they do not have to fit into the scope of anyone else's logic or judgment. To know them is to know yourself, intimately.

Journal Prompt: Reflection

Reading what I have written allows me to revisit past memories and reflections when I need to. Grieving is not a process that can be rushed, time and reflection are essential for healing. Revisiting my past can give me peace of mind and a sense of restoration. Writing allows me to give memories and reflections permanence.

Do you find yourself returning to memories or find yourself reflecting on events from your past? Consider if you would like to record those memories or reflections. If so, the following prompts may help you begin.

Begin as though you are a storyteller familiarizing an audience with your past. Expand on the details that are most important to you.

Begin in the middle of an event and work backwards explaining what led up to the event.

Write as though you are conversing with someone. A conversation can move in any direction you choose.

Journal Prompt: Each Loss is Unique

Each loss is as unique as the individual conceived. You may be able to expand on how you feel and your reasons for feeling the way you do.

When someone says, "I know just how you feel," I want to say...

Dear Reader,

"Emotional scorecard," is the phrase I chose to describe the practice of quickly judging and dismissing another person's experience. I experienced the "evaluation" numerous times following my miscarriages. Until I could put the words on paper, I could not sufficiently describe the hurt caused by the passing judgment of such a personal experience. The quick assessment did not take into account the potential of a deeper personal bond between a parent and their unborn child or consider that miscarriage severed the physical connection to life that conception established.

Journal Entry: Emotional Scorecard

My friend kept a scorecard just inside his ear. It was there so he could quickly gauge the appropriate emotional response to any given situation. As he asked me questions about my experience he would tick off my score.

You had a miscarriage? tick
It was early in your pregnancy? tick
How far along were you...ten weeks and later thirteen? tick
You never saw or heard the beating heart? tick
The ultra sound showed no form inside the sack? tick
You never actually saw a baby? tick
The surgery was out-patient? tick
Would you say the surgery was about the same or worse than a root canal? tick
You were back on you feet just hours later? tick
Pain killers or no pain killers? tick
The doctor said you can wait and try again? tick
How old are you? tick
Statistics say the odds are in your favor? tick
Your mother had how many children? tick
He knew someone who... tick

After a quick tally, a matter of simple addition and subtraction, my emotional scorecard was complete. I did not rate high enough to be allowed to grieve. It was not a real loss in his mind. Logic states if I could not see my baby, I should not miss my baby. He believed an intense emotional response following a miscarriage must not be mistaken for love or grief since hormones can do such funny things to the emotions. Once the hormones level off, the outlook should improve. My scorecard was tucked away in his memory to be recalled and held before me if ever I broached the subject again. A quick reminder of my rating would stifle any thoughts on the subject of grief and steer me back to the path of denial. Such was the case until their miscarriage occurred; my friend and his wife suffered a loss. His friend brought up a fresh scorecard to evaluate their experience.

You say you and your wife had a miscarriage? tick
How long had the two of you tried to become pregnant? tick
You say you and your wife were how far along when the miscarriage occurred? tick
You never actually carried the baby, your wife did? tick
His friend knew someone who... tick

When his emotional scorecard was complete, my friend did not score high enough to be allowed to grieve. Logic states if he did not actually carry his baby, he should not miss his baby. My friend reached out to me. He tore up my scorecard. He listened to me with an open heart rather than a mind well versed in logic. He let me express my love for my baby. My tears were allowed, accepted. I grieve as I have all along but no longer alone.

The parting of my baby from me was personal, painful and perhaps no one else will fully understand, but I will not deny the notable juncture at which we met. I honor my life. I honor the lives of my husband and my children. I honor you my babies, who stayed briefly and then were gone. I will not let someone else's quick assessment of my experiences have a defining influence. No one else experienced you in the same way I experienced you. I will take the time to mark our notable juncture in my heart and in my memory. I will stitch a quilt. I will plant a seed in the earth to grow in your memory. I will put words on paper that will yellow with age. Those words will age with me, marking the importance of you and me and our shared existence. I will take time to fold in satin and lace the memory and lay you to rest with dignity and grace. For my life has meaning and so does yours, you touched me deeply. My life may be a flash in the passing of time, but I will hold this moment for you and me; your life was short but possessed such power to move me. The loss of you has left a void; I have experienced life with you, and now I must learn to be without you.

There is a question being debated, were you tissue or were you life? You were a gift from one who bestows life. If I honor Him, I honor His gift. I have learned that the power of the gift makes the parting difficult because the love of the Giver is in His gift. The love of the Giver does remain even when the gift is no longer in my keeping; I feel it.

With your passing I was consumed by fear and anger. I have a choice to make since I could nurture any or all of these emotions in your memory. Fear of the future and losses to come. Anger at your passing and my own vulnerability. It remains a struggle to abandon the fear and anger. I must remember that the love remains with me to nurture and share. Those who receive it, will be receiving the gift of you.

E.B.

Journal Prompt: A Parting Gift

As a parting gift to my sister and my babies, I felt love was the best gift I had to offer. In my own time, I presented words of love in my journal as my farewell. Knowing they go with this gift gives me peace.

The idea of an acknowledgment of parting may be something different for you. Consider if you would like to create something tangible or present in some form, a parting gift. Preserving a memory that has some symbolic meaning can fill the need to remain connected with the one you miss or grieve.

Reflect on the following prompts to see if they present anything meaningful for you:

In parting, I choose to offer...
(You may find that your words express all that you would like to present in parting.)

Knowing you go with this gift gives me peace...
(continue if you would like to describe a gift that comes to mind)

Silent reflection is also a beautiful and meaningful expression for any time you wish and as often as you wish.

Journal Prompt: Your Life is Important to Me

The following is an invitation to write if the statement holds meaning for you.

Your life is important to me, and this is why...

Dear Reader,

The following entry was a personal observation written from the depths of depression. It served as a turning point for me by allowing me to see myself as two women. One woman held the intense emotion pulling me further into the depths capable of destroying my life. The other woman maintained hope, the strength to endure, and the desire to move through the depression to find a way to live again. I realized I needed to support her and help her find her way.

Journal Entry: The Blaze

When remembering the babies she has lost, thinking about the future and sensing a hopelessness surrounding her dreams, she thinks it would be wonderful not to hurt as she does. She has learned when you dream with all your heart and the dream dies, that part of the heart dies with it. She understands now how it is possible to die of a broken heart. One loses the will to live because life itself is governed by the heart. She imagines the relief of going to sleep and not ever again awakening to the sadness and pain. The frustration alone is unbearable, not being able to make things right. To die would be so satisfying because it is the only way she knows of to kill the pain.

She is losing her grip. The strength she has carried within is almost gone. She tries to endure each loss and disappointment and stifle the fire that is burning within but she is losing the struggle. It is beating her. You see, she is battling herself. The anger, fear, and frustration are kept within because there is nowhere to vent the emotions that have become so strong. She does not blame God, He has not brought her troubles to her. She sees her doctors as two intelligent, compassionate and gentle people who are doing everything they can to help her. She is not angry with them. Her miscarriages have been attributed to an auto-immune disorder, a situation considered rare from a medical standpoint. The technology to help her is very expensive; it is possible that it has not even been developed yet. As a result, her fear and frustration grow and there is nowhere to direct the anger, so she holds it within hoping time will dull its intensity or her situation will change and free her. It is like trying to smother a blaze but the blaze continues to increase in intensity and every blanket she produces to throw over it becomes scorched and eventually adds to the flame. Her defenses have dwindled to the extent that she does not know if she will be standing tomorrow.

She is tired. She is sad. She is disillusioned. She has not fallen as often or as hard as she has in the past nine months. Her strength is very definitely being put to the test and sometimes it seems there will be nothing left to see her through this. With every fall she loses a part of herself. She can look behind her and see the parts that have been chipped away. Some as though by a well-aimed and heavy hand that has broken through to the deepest part of her. Some as though by a careless hand that doesn't give much thought to the direction of its chisel or to the depth of its blow. The intensity of each blow feels the same to her now. It is hard to distinguish one from the other anymore. She is searching for a brace, something or someone to support her because she does not know what will be left of her when the pieces are swept away. Some have reached out to her only to pull away when she starts to fall again. It has been hard for her to tell which supports are strong enough to allow her to lean on them. She has decided that it is best to quickly cut those ties that will not hold so if she falls again, she will not risk taking anyone with her. Instead, she will turn back inside herself to the strength that is still there and hold tightly to her one true support.

She is learning about herself. She is seeing herself in a different light. She hates the woman she sometimes sees. She looks into her woman's eyes and reflected there are all her darkest emotions. At those times she fantasizes about letting go. If she did, the flame would have no place to burn. At other times, she sees a different woman. In her face she sees the sadness but also hope reflected in her tears. Her strength is being sapped but she hangs on because to let go would allow her dark side to possess her. She struggles to keep from being consumed by the blaze. She has felt the flames, they have stripped her to the extent that the purest part of her will soon be exposed. Perhaps then we will see her greatest strength; if not, she will surely die and with her all the gentleness she once possessed.

E.B.

Journal Prompt: Omniscient Observer

Imagine you are standing outside yourself as an omniscient observer. Now for the real challenge, you are both observer and subject. A personal observation can sometimes provide insight that has been overlooked. Describing yourself and your situation in the third person may enable you to look closer at aspects that might otherwise be ignored. Applaud your efforts; it may be difficult to take such a scrutinizing look. It can be disturbing at times, but it can also allow you to become reacquainted with yourself in ways that might otherwise be missed.

Describe yourself in the third person. Like a narrator in a story, describe the physical attributes of this character. Read and interpret thoughts and emotions. What is this person thinking and feeling? How would you put those ideas and feelings into words? If it makes sense to do so, provide a detailed setting as a backdrop to enhance your perception: Where is this character? Describe the physical surroundings this character sees. Consider if those surroundings in any way influence how this character thinks or feels. Do the surroundings provide you, the narrator, with further insight into the mind of this character?

Journal Prompt: Addressing Fear and Other Sources of Discomfort

Consider if the phrase "I am afraid of..." holds any meaning for you. If so, you may be able to specifically state what you fear. After stating your fears, move on to the exercise on the following page.

You may find that you experience a sense that may or may not be considered "fear" and is not specific, but presents itself in a way that causes stress, concern, or some other form of discomfort. If so, hold that thought and move on to the exercise on the following page.

Journal Prompt: Mental Exercise

The following exercise encourages you to view your fears or that unknown stress from a new perspective.

Choose one of your fears or allow the stress to come forward for now. Personify it by giving it a name. Describe it as though it has facial features and a physical stature. (It does not have to be human in appearance or form.) What capabilities does this inflated figure possess? How does its presence affect you? Let your imagination flow. Now tell what capabilities are within your grasp to deflate this fearful or distressing figure. Finally, imagine and describe your empowered self standing confidently over the crumpled mass.

Dear Reader,

I wondered what my future could hold when the grief of loss was all-consuming. I questioned whether I was capable of experiencing happiness again. During life's lowest points, the concept of bliss can be a difficult concept to digest. I tried to digest the concept of bliss and instead choked on it. The trick is to take it in small doses, bliss is then possible to ingest and you receive the full benefits.

Journal Entry: Bliss?

As a well-known expert in the field of mythology, Joseph Campbell also earned recognition as a professor, philosopher and theologian. The following is advice Campbell offered to his students seeking counsel concerning their lifelong pursuits: *"Follow your bliss, go where body and soul want to go. When you follow your bliss, you come to bliss."* The advice exhibits Campbell's optimism in the individual's ability to seek and find happiness but seems misleading and naive. I believe a more accurate projection would warn that unforeseen circumstances can greatly influence lives and emphasize that the individual must be capable of finding bliss in everyday situations. True bliss must be nurtured from within the individual.

According to *The American Heritage Dictionary-New College Edition,* Bliss is defined as: 1. "Serene happiness" 2. "The ecstasy of salvation" 3. "A cause of great delight or happiness." If by bliss, Campbell refers to happiness, the implication is that the individual has only to follow the body's urges and instincts to find happiness. The body, however, is not always a reliable guide. The body is susceptible to chemical addictions that wrongly give the impression of elation or bliss but in reality can lead to misery or death. Overeating can seem blissful until it leads to obesity. It could be argued that sexual assaults can be attributed to some extent, to individuals wrongly following the urges of the body. Domestic violence is difficult to combat when a victim believes love is present in the relationship and refuses to leave a dangerous situation. Love is commonly attributed to the workings of body and soul. In a situation where domestic violence is present, going where body and soul want to go may lead to tragedy rather than bliss.

"When you follow your bliss, you come to bliss." I assume that in this portion of his statement, Campbell is referring to both happiness and salvation. His intended meaning being perhaps, that when you follow your salvation, you come to happiness. Another possible interpretation could be, when you follow your happiness, you come to salvation. Leeming's book on mythology illustrates the fact that not everyone has the luxury to choose the direction they will take in life. Heracles from Greek myth, was a victim of a spell that led him to murder his family. To make amends, Heracles was ordered by the gods to serve King Eurystheus. He was forced to complete twelve great tasks to attain salvation. Heracles faced extreme danger in completing the tasks and when his beloved mentor was killed by Heracles' arrow, Heracles experienced incredible sorrow. Heracles' eventual salvation was a result of his strength in facing extreme challenges, undaunted by fear or sorrow. Happiness did not play a significant role in the life of Heracles.

Phrygian myth tells of the boy Attis who did seek happiness. Attis sought to marry the daughter of King Midas. His plans were waylaid by Agdistis, who prevented the marriage from taking place because of his love for Attis. In anger, Attis castrated himself and died. Myth provides numerous examples of the influence of life's challenges. Those who hope to follow body and soul to bliss may be disillusioned by the inevitable burden of responsibility in supporting themselves, maintaining relationships and dealing with the setbacks that life dishes out.

The Chinese myth Kuan Yin, describes a tormented woman who is murdered by her father's servant and finds herself in the Land of the Dead. Prevented from following her desire to live her life in the temple of the White Bird, Kuan Yin overcomes her fear of death and sings to relieve the eternal sorrow that surrounds her. The king of the house of the dead banishes Kuan Yin and returns her to earth. Kuan Yin lives on an island providing comfort in the "continuing cycle of troubles that afflict all beings in the gyre of time." I believe the myth of Kuan Yin provides a more realistic perspective on life than Campbell provides with his statement. Kuan Yin demonstrates that body and soul are not always accommodated in this life and bliss must often be nurtured within the individual, regardless of one's surroundings and situation. I believe those who are capable of finding bliss in everyday situations are more likely to find salvation from circumstances and places where body and soul do not wish to be.

E.B.

Journal Prompt: Activities to Relax and Feel Rejuvenated

What activities do you enjoy that allow you to relax or feel rejuvenated?
(an activity might be as simple as closing your eyes and putting your feet up
for 10 minutes or as exerting as a game of tennis)

List five activities you enjoy on the lines below:

1. _____

2. _____

3. _____

4. _____

5. _____

**Choose one activity you enjoy and work it into your schedule. If now is not
possible, create some time for yourself before the day's end. See if you can
complete every activity on your list in the next few days. When you have
reached the end of your list, begin again or create a new list and continue to
treat yourself to at least a few minutes each day of personal attention or
meditation.**

Journal Prompt: Living With the Myriad of Emotions

I offered no apologies for my grief, nor for the emotions it evoked. The reasons for my grief were my own. I had to be the one to define my experience. But it was necessary for me to gain some perspective on my emotions and learn how best to care for myself if I felt overwhelmed or depleted.

Consider the following emotions, they are emotions that may be experienced following a loss. Reflect on how you might respond in a nurturing way to work through the emotion. Offered are some ideas that may be helpful.

I feel anger when...

I can ease the anger by...(removing myself from a situation, taking a walk, writing in my journal, listening to my favorite music, etc.)

I am overcome by sadness when...

I recognize the sadness and know it is there because...(sometimes voicing reasons for the sadness or just voicing that the sadness exists is helpful. It reaffirms what is being experienced below the surface and may ease the stirrings.)

I experience loneliness when...

When I am feeling lonely I can...(call a friend, write a note to someone I have wanted to stay in touch with, sit with or walk my pet, etc.)

I find myself frustrated when...

To ease the frustration I might...(consider a physical activity such as Yoga, walking, running, water aerobics, swimming, racquetball, etc.)

I was confused when...

I can sort through my confusion by...(talking to my doctor, searching for informative reading material to answer my questions, contacting a support organization such as Resolve or S.H.A.R.E., etc.)

I long to...

Am I longing for something presently attainable? If so, I can satisfy the longing by...(If it is not something presently attainable but something temporarily out of reach, imagine yourself attaining or accomplishing what you long to do. There is power in positive thinking. If you long for something beyond your reach, imagine yourself attaining it and send the image off like a prayer or a heartfelt vision.)

Part III

Spiritual Reflections and Dreams

Dear Reader,

Following my miscarriages, my directional slate was wiped clean. The direction I had chosen was altered by setbacks and I had to reevaluate my stance and ask some difficult questions. Sitting in a support group, the questions that arose in the minds of parents who had suffered an early infancy loss or those struggling to conceive, were not limited to thoughts of future pregnancies or infertility. The questions ran the gamut from practical to spiritual in nature. I wondered what choices were mine to make and what fate dictated. When life dishes out extreme disappointments, it is a struggle to stay centered and focused. It is common to wonder if God has abandoned me.

Journal Entry: Eve of the Soul

As I wander, how shall I choose a path?
Will my way be decided by my stumbling
To land face to face with the serpent?
Or subtly revealed in the wind's passing,
Tangling leaves across my path to indicate a direction?
Who is to blame if I make the wrong choice?
Will I be guilty, if in my ignorance I fear the serpent
And attempt an escape,
Failing to realize the fight for survival
Shucks obscure layers to reveal the vibrant core?

If I merely enjoy the cool breeze that sweeps strands across my cheek,
Or stop to appreciate the playfulness of the leaves as they dance across my path:
Chasing, teasing, tumbling, racing to be first to reach who knows where...
Have I missed my calling?
Am I to follow the whimsical example of the leaves and take up the chase,
Or is my fate intertwined with the serpent?

Does fate have the strength to hold me fixed until I see my way?
If not, how many chances will I be given if I miss my cue?
Will You search me out and bring me home?

What binds me to You once I am submerged in conceptual waters?
Bound in flesh and physically nourished gives rise to physical dominance.
The trauma of birth frees the body but silences the soul.
The body must develop and learn to conceptualize,
Only a growing awareness of that which is not physical enables the soul to thaw.
Time is a well-chosen gift.

I have yet to experience the body's bindings,
And I fear my own extinction
If I lack the strength to move within the body's limiting boundaries.
How shall I acquaint the body with the reality of Your Being?
Through what medium shall we communicate?
That is it...is it not?
Artistic fervor as a means of expression,
Serves as link composing the trinity: body, soul and Being.
Our bond remains unbroken so long as body gives voice to the soul,
Who ultimately reveals, You.

I see clearly my path.
I am prepared to go.

E.B.

Journal Prompt: Liberating Expression

The following exercise can be a liberating form of expression. Creating a dialogue can give definition to those aspects of your experience that need to be voiced but may not be the expressions you wish to share with another person at this time, or ever. Following a loss, it is not unusual to be bombarded by thoughts that we may or may not embrace. Expressing them is for the personal benefit of bringing to the forefront those conflicting ideas that can continue to be a disruptive force to you personally, until they are voiced in some form. Once voiced, you will be free to keep them if they prove to be a meaningful extension of you, or discard them as you see fitting.

Create a dialogue with someone you feel a need to speak to...
Talk to God.
Talk to the "voice of reason."
Talk to the one for whom you are grieving.
Talk to Mother Earth.
Talk to the sky.
Talk to a cloud, the sun, a star.
Talk and listen.
Follow wherever your thoughts lead.

It may be easier to follow the dialogue if you write down what you wish to say. As you do, listen for thoughtful responses and record everything you say and hear...

Dear Reader,

Frustration mounted as I searched for the cause of my miscarriages. Frustration turned to anger when I encountered those who misunderstood my grief and wanted me to rush through the grief and return to my former self. Those who failed to recognize the importance of my babies' lives or denied their existence, trampled on sacred ground. The bond I experienced with my babies during my pregnancies is undeniable. The loss of life due to miscarriage and the idea conveyed to me that miscarriage is not a loss to be taken seriously, led me to examine my own beliefs about love, loss, and the hereafter. In a sense, I experienced a spiritual grief as I struggled to understand my own misfortune and to clarify my beliefs about the significance of life, both long-lived and briefly held. I explored reasons for our existing and dying and renewed my understanding of God's presence. The loss of miscarriage became the cornerstone of a deep spiritual exploration that proved to be personally nurturing.

Journal Entry: The Joining

Is there an afterlife...a heaven and hell? What happens to us when our physical presence is no more? What is love and how should it be expressed? What is the reason for our being on this earth? Do you ever attempt to answer these questions for yourself? I do. My answers seem contradictory if the fine line is not considered. The fine line more keenly defines these concepts that elude me. That line I am learning is what ties these questions and concepts together to make them one and the same in my mind. While listening to a discussion of these topics, the questions that stayed with me were: Why would God create such an imperfect world? If He is God and capable of creating perfection, why is it we could probably all offer suggestions to Him on how to improve this place...suggestions on how to create a "more perfect world?" The idea that comes to my mind is that we don't know what God's reasons were for creating this world. This world for all we know meets God's objectives perfectly. If I view the earth as a vessel that carries us and sustains us through this temporary existence, the idea of a perfect world, in my mind is too permanent, unnecessary for a temporary state. This is a world of constant change, both growth and decay occur within this temporary state. The vessel itself is aging. Science speculates the earth had a definite and profound beginning in the distant past and is destined for an eventual end. If that is the case, there is a parallel between the vessel earth and the human body.

Everything physical is subject to change that seems to result eventually in varying stages of "decay," yet certain aspects of our humanity seem to maintain a repetition that is a recognizable pattern. The studies of anthropology, history, and biology, as a sampling, have revealed both social patterns of humanity and physical patterns of our humanness. Humanity has left a powerful imprint in spite of the fragility of life and an unstable and deteriorating bodily presence. The legacy establishes that our aging physical presence is not all there is to us. Consider the human essence or soul within the body like the legacy of humanity, growing, developing, expanding and evolving. Consider too that elements of that essence might be expressed through applied intelligence, physical abilities and other talents. This temporary state presents innumerable obstacles and challenges, and apart from being extremely frustrating at times, it does serve to foster intellectual, emotional, and spiritual growth.

Are we meant to improve as we experience the changes in this temporary world or are we challenged to avoid change in order to maintain a childlike innocence? An argument could be developed to support either idea. Some might argue that the innocent state of a child is far better than the cynicism of an adult. But if an adult's cynicism is based on outrage at the injustices and inconsistencies of this changing world, the resulting cynicism can be interpreted as an intelligent and reasonable response. The fine line is drawn where cynicism has the effect of halting growth by disabling or stunting one intellectually, spiritually, or emotionally.

The innocent phases of a child's growth naturally move from the purely physical to the abstract. I have watched a baby discover his toes and listened to a child read stories to her stuffed animals as they sat together on the "potty." Yesterday, she sat in a chair happily counting her hiccups. The phases are becoming more complex; my son asked me today how I knew there was a God. "If He is everywhere and in everyone, how would He do that?" His thinking and exploration has moved from the physical to the infinite.

In my allegory, God was the sculptor, an artist who put a part of Himself into each piece He created. All of us, having been formed by His hand possess a vestige of Him. He put a part of Himself in you, I said to my son. He hopes you will cultivate the gift He has placed in your keeping so you can present it to the world. Nurturing brings it forth. Once you make a conscious effort to nurture the essence within, you will sense His presence. That is when you will know God exists. An established artist develops a distinct style. A single piece can be identified among a row of pieces by numerous artists by the unique style of the artist who created it. You will be recognized by the Artist; He sees His work through each stage of development and will know the final product.

An appreciation of the artist's deep love for his piece can result from the luxury of time...but how should this love be expressed? By definition, love can range from "God's benevolence and mercy toward man," to "an intense sexual desire for another person." (Morris) The sexual expression of love is of vast importance as it is essential for the continuation of our species, but it seems the most primitive and at the lowest level of love's capacity. Yet the miracle of life that results from the physical expression of love gives a sense of the enormity and power of God's love...love at its highest level. A level of love that exceeds the physical expression is experienced when individuals create a bond that strengthens and protects, allowing growth to occur from within. Both individuals become a truer vision of their being. (Another lame attempt to describe something too vast for words.) The word is hardly adequate to describe the emotion and experience of love in all its forms. It is too simplistic a name for a force that touches the many aspects of our lives and is directed toward so many in our lives.

As we grow and learn about ourselves and others in this world, we can glimpse the precious essence and strength of each individual. We can appreciate the gift of life as we tap its potential but it is beyond our ability to realize all the ramifications of our existence. The fine line trips us up when we try to explain in concrete terms the results of creation from our limited perspective or specifically define God's Being. When I was much younger, I read a passage by C.S. Lewis. If I am remembering clearly, he described a circle of souls who couldn't find God even though God was reaching out and calling to them. They were paralyzed in their fear and could not hear His voice or feel His touch. I pictured their afterlife devoid of any joining with God, their experience beyond this earth like a black hole, cold and dark, devoid of love. The tragedy of ignorance, fear, and hatred, is evident when an individual becomes engulfed and stifled in the smothering cocoon.

It is inevitable that the body or soul's receptacle will gradually wear away to release its contents into the unknown. So what of our being when our physical presence is no longer possible to sustain? Is there heaven and hell? I don't see a heaven that is a perfect earth where we continue our lives without pain and so experience "perfect happiness." Nor do I see fire and brimstone. I do believe in an afterlife. When asked what becomes of the soul after death, a Jewish Rabbi replied, the soul is not a physical presence and so it can not die, it just is. It continues to be. I also believe in the continuance of the soul. So what of all those we have loved? I believe there is a joining after we die, a melding of souls and all the individual gifts, intelligence, and love, that God has bestowed on each individual. When rejoined with God's Being, the force created is perfection realized.

E.B.

Journal Prompt: Record Your Thoughts

Pause for reflection, you may wish to record your thoughts.

Dear Reader,

The following entry resulted through the reasoning and exploration of a period in my life when I felt overwhelmed and powerless to find answers for all the "whys" and to bring about outcomes I personally desired. Following the loss of my baby, I felt stripped and empty. Wanting my baby so badly, my life seemed stunted. An essential part of our family was missing. Unable to sustain my baby's life, I felt my body had betrayed me. In my grief and sorrow and overshadowing depression, I lost sight of my own worth. Bringing a new life into the world is a wondrous gift but it is essential not to forget that you, yes you, are a living gift, unique, fascinating, and valuable.

Journal Entry: Being Ordinary

There are days I am overwhelmed by the realization of being ordinary. It hits me with a jolt. Something nearing panic, leads me to believe I must pack my bag in search of anything, just so it be less ordinary! I scan my life and the images on the timeline are composed and completed with such brevity. How is it possible to feel so old and so young in the same instant? I shift my footing to test the steadiness of this place, this space I occupy. It seems solid, real. Then the questions flood my mind. Why am I here? Do you ever feel there is something that must be accomplished before you leave this place? Yes! A vague idea of what that might be begins to shape itself in my consciousness. A sense of calm replaces the panic, soothing the needlelike pricks that extend from my chest to my fingertips. The image swirls in my consciousness, almost visible but just out of reach. I know it from somewhere so why is it so vague? Have I forgotten something essential or is the timing wrong for me to see the image crystal clear? Perhaps, but I also have a sense that the truth is a part of me, so much so that there is no reason for it to be defined, spoken.

I am bewildered by a sense of being like a grain of sand. Poetically phrased, "Like the grain of sand blown by the wind..." The image gives a sense of the power of the wind and the vulnerability of the wind's captive amidst vast surroundings. The single grain rode the currents to eventually become a child's castle, a mountain, the grit in my teeth or the speck in my eye. Why did the wind chauffeur that particular grain to its destination? Was the ride a result of fate or chance? There are as many answers to those questions as to the question: Why in my eye? After all, there were so many other places the wind could have set it. If nothing else, the necessity to remove that speck from my painfully red, tearing eye, proves to me that I am actively involved in the motion of my surroundings.

51

Examining more closely the grain of sand, are any two grains alike entirely: size, shape, color, texture? Do they all catch the light and reflect it in just the same way? In a few words, the grain of sand is no longer ordinary but profound in its basic composition.

Remember the experience as a kid, running to catch the wind as it sent sand and litter swirling into the sky? The funnel's center was the ideal spot; the sand stung my legs and the wind whipped up my skirt. Maybe you aren't the type to wear a skirt but wasn't the idea of riding the wind a thrill? It always left me breathless and sorry I could only keep up for a moment before the wind moved on without me or ended the game by allowing the sand to settle back down to earth, scattering litter across the landscape.

The landscape of my mind is composed of regions to explore. There are times I delve deeply and I am amazed at how much there is to learn. I find answers to questions I know are true, my heart tells me so. But I am left feeling childlike in my inability to grasp complete understanding from my limited perspective. For all the infinite answers to questions posed; there is still the single "Why?" I fear is beyond my ability to comprehend.

I gain some insight if I contemplate relationships and follow up with comparisons. Like the sandy shore and the single grain of sand, there exists the population of the human race and the oneness of the individual. There is the complexity of an individual and the simplicity of a single cell. It is enlightening to note similarities while recognizing relationships and making comparisons. There is then the challenge of unraveling the contradictions. Pose a question, any question. Now delve deeply to chase the possibilities, like an otter slick and lithe, twisting and turning to capture the plaything just out of reach. I discover the exercise of exploring broadens my scope, not the answer simply stated.

As through a picture window, my view of life unfolds before me. No one will see through the panes that border my world at precisely the same angle. It is a view uniquely my own. Nor can I view the world from another's perspective. My view and their's is skewed. We can stand side by side and describe the setting before us, but the details will vary. The scenes may overlap, but our interpretations of those scenes will not be identical; they cannot be. We have experiences that broaden our understanding of people, places, and events, but we still have borders to contend with. I wonder why the borders are there. They exist for what purpose? Are those panes that limit my view real or imagined?

Excluding the world beyond the picture window, directing my focus inward, my shortcomings become all too clear. The multitude frightens me and at times I have to turn away. If courageously I persist in drawing the curtains to the outside world, an inner world, both vast and spiritual is revealed. Within the individual resides a presence possessing strength and vision. As I come to know and honor this presence, I begin to value the panes for defining more deeply who

I am. That which blocks my view of the world, captures within its borders the essence of me. That oneness is who I am.

We may appear ordinary if our focus is the world outside, and we reflect on the span of time we spend here and the subtle changes the average individual seems to bring to the world. Refuse to simply view the world, but nurture instead the presence within and reflect it back to the world. Each individual is an integral part of this world possessing a tremendous capacity to enrich this place.

Is a single star special if it is a tiny essence among billions? In other words, if a star is one among billions reflecting in the night sky, is its value diminished? It is the billions reflecting in number that creates the view that is breathtaking. If one star stands alone does it lose the ability, without the others, to captivate us? Remove all other stars from view so only one is visible through the blackness; would we be able to turn away? What was commonplace is now exceptional. We are enticed to explore the phenomenon, for a solitary star creates vivid contrast to the emptiness. The night sky is vast and would seem hollow, empty, but for the reflections of the stars to make it distinctly visible, memorable. One among billions, a single star reflects and adds to the splendor of the night. An ordinary individual, one among billions, is a treasure worth revealing.

E.B.

Journal Prompt: Love and Tenderness

While grieving it is healing to remember that we are all deserving of love and tenderness. We must continue to love and nurture ourselves.

From a personal perspective, how would you complete the following prompt?

These are 5 qualities, abilities or attributes, I am happy to possess:

1. _____

2. _____

3. _____

4. _____

5. _____

How have these personal characteristics enriched your life and the lives of those around you?

Journal Prompt: Connect With Yourself

Connect with yourself,
Be creative,
Be honest,
Be bold,
Be a child,
Search,
Question,
Wonder,
Be the teacher,
Be the pupil,
Be thoughtful,
Be yourself,
Freely.

This exercise can help you become centered and focused amid the distractions of the day. Experience being in this place in time. Explore with your senses. Try to experience the rhythm of your surroundings. In observing your surroundings, notice objects, colors, textures, smells, etc. Include a physical description of yourself in these surroundings. Consider your mood at the present, reflect on passing thoughts.

Write about today, here, now:

Here I sit, pen in hand...

Journal Entry: The Dream

I had a dream last night. It was the first dream I can remember having since my miscarriages. I was walking down a breezeway with a friend of mine. I don't remember a name or a face but I felt very close to this friend, whoever it was. I was carrying two eggs. One was twice the size of a chicken's egg and I cupped it gently in my left hand. The one I held in my right hand was smaller, it was the size of a chicken's egg. My friend and I were looking at these eggs as we walked through the breezeway. Between the buildings it was dark and so it was hard to see the eggs clearly. They looked ordinary except for the difference in size. The white shells shone in the dark. I was telling my friend that they felt smooth to touch but the shells were so delicate I could feel the impression my thumb left as though I had pressed it against a ball of wet clay. I asked my friend what would become of these eggs and whether there was likely to be anything living inside them. We both seemed to agree they were too fragile to be able to sustain a life long enough for it to develop beyond the egg. We were going to discard the eggs. I don't know why, except we had no use for them. I remember thinking it was a shame they were so useless. I was curious about what they might have produced.

As we reached the end of the breezeway, the sun was shining. As we walked beyond the shadow of the last building into the sunshine, the eggs changed. Gradually both of them became translucent. They felt warm to touch and when I held them up to the light I could see inside them. In each egg there was a dark form suspended in what appeared to be clear gel. The form was not one I could recognize. It looked about the size and shape of a lima bean; it had the same smooth edges. There didn't seem to be any movement at first...but then I felt it. It was so slight, I thought I had imagined it. There was a quick flutter that came and went. I froze when I felt it so I could be sure not to miss it if it came again. It did come again but much stronger this time and it did not disappear. The movement could be felt but it could not be seen. I recognized the movement. I had felt it before. I wanted my friend to feel it too, but I was afraid the eggs were too fragile to be moved. My friend asked me to describe what I felt, so I tried to describe how the eggs seemed to gently throb in my hands. The best way to describe it was like a baby moving in the womb. Some women liken the movement to being lightly brushed by a butterfly's wings. I always thought the movement felt like fins brushing by me in the water. The excitement I felt was the same as I had experienced the first time I felt my baby move. It was the assurance that my baby was really there.

Suddenly these eggs were of value to me because of the life being sustained within the delicate shells. I did not want to discard them anymore. I knew I had to. It seemed like such a waste. I could feel the tears in my eyes. My friend looked at me and understood. With an arm around me, we walked to the place where we had to leave the eggs. It was a grassy area next to a pond of dirty water. When I set the eggs in the grass, I was very careful not to disturb them. I stood up and moved next to my friend. We were both watching the eggs. The eggs broke open, and we caught just a glimpse of what was inside them. The larger egg opened first. A bright orange fish lay in the grass for just a second beside the broken egg until it flipped itself into the water. A white fish came from the smaller egg and it immediately reached the water and swam away.

My friend and I were so excited we were jumping up and down. For the first time we realized we had been so absorbed in what was happening with the eggs, we had not noticed all the people sitting in the sun around the water. They were all looking at us. There was a man sitting close to us so we tried to explain what had happened. He didn't seem to appreciate the significance of the eggs. He didn't seem interested at all. Nobody did.

My own feelings were of relief. I knew I was not responsible for the eggs. They were not dependent on me. Even after I had discarded them, the life inside them continued to change and grow and eventually live independently of the egg. My dream ended there. I had tears in my eyes like I usually do when I wake up now, but these were different. I woke up for the first time feeling rested and happy...really happy.

I want to remember this dream because it holds something for me that I have not been able to grasp for months. I often try to picture what the cells in my body looked like before they disintegrated and were washed away. I want to see the eggs containing the multiplying cells that would have been my babies if only the condition of my body or the make-up of the cells had been different. I want to look inside the eggs and count how many times they had divided. I wish I knew why and just when they stopped growing, but I guess I never will. My doctor first referred to them as nothing. "There was nothing there," but then he agreed there was life. He knew it and I knew it. In fact, I will not accept anything else.

What I think about now is the soul. When is a life granted a soul? Is it as a baby takes its first breath or perhaps when life is conceived? I hope it is with conception so even if a life lasts for only a moment, its value will not be denied in the eyes of God. I want to know that those lives were not wasted just because they were not able to stay with me long enough to take that first breath or take on a more human form. Some people can draw a line and once

57

development reaches that line, the life is recognized. Some people think it is when a fetus has facial features and recognizable limbs. Others see it when development is complete and the baby is just putting on weight before birth. I cannot draw a line since even the sperm lives and dies. I guess it is the value each of us places on that life that is debatable. I cannot say my own life is any more valuable than the ones I lost because I do not know what qualities or characteristics they would have possessed. I believe that God did not intend for us to act as judge in matters we cannot fully understand. That is why I choose to respect each life, however short, because I see each one existing as a result of God's creation. Maybe that is the answer I have been searching for. Maybe it is not a question of when a soul is introduced. Maybe the soul was a concept that was introduced to help us understand our own importance in the eyes of God. The intent being, to help us understand the value God has placed on each one of us as His children; something that once granted, can never be taken away. God knows the true value of each life. Each life is a gift full of promise and though short-lived, can have some impact; just as the two lives that came and left so suddenly have had a tremendous impact on me.

E.B.

Journal Prompt: Dreams

Dreams often help us put in order our thoughts when emotion claims our ability to reason. Is there a dream that has left a lasting impression, been visually memorable, or emotionally calming?

Reflect on the images of a dream. To preserve the dream images, draw them as pictures or describe them with words.

I dreamt...

Journal Entry: Tiny Life

Tiny life enfolded in Mother's womb,
Changing, growing, becoming whole.
Encased in a delicate sack, nourished, nurtured.
The result of a joining.
In love or not,
Given time to be...a miracle.
Always a miracle, valued or not.

The beat of a heart.
The essence of God made visible, resounding.
Another joining, love promised from Him, thus received.
Tiny life, tiny limbs.
What do you hear?
What do you feel?
Beating heart provides mother's warmth.
Sincerely or not,
The difference is not yet realized.

Born to this world.
Encased in this tiny being;
Intelligence and abilities lay hidden.
God's view, unrevealed.
Will we be wise enough to raise this child?
Are we capable of laboring again
To bring forth the individual within?
Tiny child, we labor for you
But you must take up the fight.
As you journey forth, buffeted, bruised,
Draw strength from God's breath which gave you life.

Nearly grown, you choose the path.
Another promise bestowed.
The responsibility at times, daunting.

"Fully grown," marvel at the miracle.
Embrace the experience.
Savor what remains.
Tomorrow, your passing.
What will you hear?
What will you feel?
God's ageless whisper.
Beckoned by a kiss.
Drawn forth eternally,
Changing, growing, becoming whole.

E.B.

Journal Prompt: Record Your Thoughts

Pause for reflection, you may wish to record your thoughts.

Dear Reader,

My reflections often return to the mysteries of miscarriage and what came to pass as a result of my inability to sustain the lives that were once growing and changing within me. It is not easy for a mother and father to accept that one day their baby was present through pregnancy and now there is "nothing there." My questioning and exploration always lead me to consider the spiritual aspect of our existence.

Journal Entry: The Departure

Reflecting on a dream, I recall how I stood on the shore and watched them go. Those departing souls vanished like water evaporating from a scorching hot surface. The wet outline was visible, the moisture I could touch. I watched as the wet shape changed, enthralled that something could move from one form to another before my eyes and then vanish so completely from sight. Departing souls, once tangible, were now vaporous. I reluctantly released those souls to the unknown, knowing full-well they had a place to go. It was a destination I longed for myself. Perhaps I even envied their timing. Being so young and new, they succeeded in avoiding life's fray. Venturing to ponder the advantages to an early departure, I had also to acknowledge life's responsibilities left unfinished. What had they left behind incomplete? Relationships might now be without the essential partner to make them whole, aside from the void left in me. I envisioned missing pieces in a colorful and complex jigsaw puzzle. Lives that would have connected with others had departed leaving those awaiting untouched.

The painful surge emerged from deep within me when I pondered the world without their touch, their sounds, the marks that would have been expressions of their souls. This is the source of my grief. The world seemed stripped and empty. Essential elements were missing. The world had been cheated in reaching its depth. The world or humanity? The world nurtures humanity so both seemed to have been cheated. Each was a life leaving a lifetime unfulfilled, at least that is the way it seemed from where I stood. Until I considered that water turning to vapor is an essential step in a life sustaining cycle. Eventually the rain returns so that life may continue. In this case however I am the sole survivor, the only one to embrace their existence. But no, my friend knew too of whom I speak. Together we grieved from today's departure but joyously celebrated tomorrow's glory.

E.B.

Journal Prompt: Reflecting on a Dream

Once again, reflect on an evoking dream. The thoughts and emotions that come to mind as you recall details of the dream can be a source of inspiration and personal insight. It can be beneficial to record the accompanying thoughts and emotions, leaving you free to examine them closely or to simply remember what this dream evoked in you.

Reflecting on a dream I recall...

Part IV

The Power of Remembrance

Dear Reader,

I learned the invaluable lesson of remembering from a friend who lost her son. She shared her memories with me and taught me that not even death could sever her relationship with her son. The journal entries, "Teardrop" and "Mother's Remembrance," were inspired by the insight she lovingly shared with me. Her words and friendship continue to lend me strength and lighten my load.

Journal Entry: Mother's Remembrance

On my way out to run errands, I stopped to check the mail. I sat in the car and thumbed through the envelopes. Coming across a letter, I tore it open and read it in the car. It was a letter from a friend. I had never visited the site of her son's accident. My friend took me there seven years after her son's passing, adeptly using words on paper. I have learned not to fight the tears anymore. They flowed freely as I walked through the day with her. I was with her through that period when the emotions began to surface and there was something to know, something to understand about the moment. The overwhelming sense made everyday events seem empty, misplaced somehow. The fatigue soon followed. Perhaps the fatigue came from the effort of her heart and soul straining to communicate with her consciousness amid all the distractions and responsibilities of daily life. When she gave in to it and rested, the search began in earnest.

I looked closely with her as she pointed out the scene of his accident. The pieces of glass and the chips of paint, there against the rough texture of the soil; all visible in my mind's eye. I noted with her the inevitable change, the wider road and smoother soil left the impression of time's quick passing. Ironically the road changed and yet time stood still. The surrounding desert vista, calm and serene at its best, cradled the memory. Looking into the sun amid the yellow-orange sky, there was the sense of God's presence and with Him, her son. I saw her son's face, happy and confident. I recognized his beautiful, playful smile. I sensed the bond between mother and son melded tightly for eternity, such strength the two of them possess. My heart swelled and ached in celebration of the love of mother for her son. We walked away from that place, she and I, but we will never leave it.

Remembrance illuminates the essence her son reflected to the world. Thank you my friend for allowing me to share the gift of your son's love with you. It is a love I deeply respect and honor. There is such joy amid the sorrow. God's gift, fully embraced and treasured is at times almost too painful to bear. Relinquishing the honor of holding His gift in exchange for pain's release is tenaciously rejected by her, for she is Mother in its purest sense. Her reward is God and her son, in her life for all eternity.

E.B.

Journal Prompt: Remember Sources of Comfort

If there are those whose words or gestures have been a source of comfort and inspiration, remember them.

It helped me when...

Dear Reader,

In my reading, I came across the following comment. It held a special meaning for me. My thoughts immediately returned to the poem, "Teardrop."

"As I sit across from my analysand I raise the question: 'This space that is between you and me—is it a space that separates us one from the other, or is it a space that unites us one to the other?' The answer, clearly, is that it is both or either, depending upon the way we choose to look at it."

June Singer
Boundaries Of The Soul

Journal Entry: Teardrop

In the shower, fully revealed.
The voice of reason questions.
Why this grief after so long?
Why not let go and move on?
Do you not trust they are in His keeping?

It is not a matter of my trusting or not trusting God,
I say to the droplet magnifying the curtain before me.
I experience their absence even as I celebrate their existence.
Not forfeit, they remain
Fastened through the heart.
We live and we love forever...
Tearlike, the drop letdown the curtain,
Reducing the image of the barrier that divides me.

E.B.

Journal Prompt: What is Left for Me to Keep?

I invite you to complete the thought and continue writing if the following statements are meaningful to you.

"Your left me but I did not want you to go. Too much has been left unshared. What is left for me to keep? What memories are mine to hold?"

When I think of you and the time we were together, I remember...

Part V

Strategies for Confronting Stress

Journal Entry: Another Chance

Following the diagnosis of an auto-immune disorder, we attempted two more pregnancies. It became necessary to begin injections of the anticoagulant, heparin to prevent clotting around the placenta. Administered within forty-eight hours of ovulation, the injections were necessary until two weeks prior to delivery. The heparin injections twice a day became easier with practice. I found them to be less painful when taken in the abdomen than in my thighs and the bruising to be less if I carefully applied constant pressure rather than jabbing the needle in quickly. I was also directed to take a dose of baby aspirin daily. Prolonged morning sickness and stress made both pregnancies difficult. Although at times the morning sickness was reassuring in making me feel very pregnant; I was fortunate to have my mom's lifesaving meatballs. They were the only food I was able to keep down for several months. A meal consisted of two or three small meatballs. I still remember the queasiness as I sat staring at those monotonous meatballs on the plate.

David was three when I was pregnant with Morgan. The first time he found me being sick, he threw open the bathroom door and shouted, "Mommy! What's wrong, is the baby stuck in your throat?" Later he would reassure anyone who was unfortunate enough to be around when I was sick: "Oh that's just Mom, she does that all the time." When I dropped David off at preschool, he would usually turn to me and say, "Get some rest Mom, and try to eat something." At those times he seemed so much older than three. He brought home bags of rocks, twigs and leaves from his nature walks at school and set them by my bed so I would have something nice to look at when I was not feeling well. I was well cared for by David and Peter, my husband.

I was fortunate in being able to eventually receive the medical attention required to give birth to two more healthy babies. Both pregnancies were monitored closely with non-stress tests and ultrasounds. I was relieved my baby's growth was being watched so closely because it seemed for months my baby's diet consisted of heparin, aspirin, and meatballs. Morgan was delivered full term with no complications. In the beginning of the eighth month of carrying Vanessa, the placenta started to tear away causing a drop in the amniotic fluid. An amniocentesis indicated her lungs were not fully developed. A second amniocentesis a week later, showed she could be delivered safely. She was five pounds, fourteen ounces, and very healthy. She was also very hungry. I was able to nurse her soon after she was born. And unlike me, she still enjoys a good meatball.

I have a very good friend who has told me she believes my children are here as a result of sheer tenacity, the result of not letting go and not giving up. Tenacity and faith helped me endure the emotional struggle. Faith was the source of gentle healing: faith in God, faith in my inner-self, faith in the gift of life. A gentle healing light shown even in the darkest corners. I can not take credit for that, I can only thank God it was there. I am relieved to look back with joy as well as sadness. I look at Vanessa smiling at me with chocolate pudding on the end of her nose and know the image is priceless. My beliefs about life and love and what is truly important to me have not changed. I am happy to be home raising my children. I have spent hours changing diapers, preparing meals, cleaning messes, reading stories, helping at school, helping with homework. All those activities may seem trite to some but make me feel like the luckiest mom in the world. I see beyond the everyday routine to the influence I have on my children. I consider myself in a privileged position. I watch my children move through the various stages of development and I am fascinated and impressed at the personalities I see unfolding, each one so different from the other. I have no dreams or preconceived ideas of what I want my children to be when they grow to adulthood. Only that they recognize their own abilities and see in themselves the intelligent, capable individuals I see. I want my children to grow strong and able to confront their world with confidence. The lessons and attitudes they learn from me will shape their lives and influence their futures, therefore; I do not take for granted this role I have been given.

E.B.

Journal Prompt: Stress/Opposing the Negative

Throughout my experiences with grief and loss, I was challenged by my own doubts, fears and vulnerabilities. Stresses stemming from my past experiences influenced the present and threatened the future. It was a continuous challenge to confront the overshadowing thoughts and emotions and prevent them from becoming a debilitating force. My therapist offered the following advice to me. For every negative thought that pushes its way into your mind, counter it with a positive thought to balance the negative, then think one more positive thought to put you again on positive footing to move ahead.

Reflect on images you find enjoyable or calming. If you were to choose an image that allowed your mind to move away from daily stresses and concerns, what might it be? If you were to create the image on paper or in some other form, would it be best conveyed with words, paint, pen and ink, watercolor, crayons, mosaic, clay, sculpture, music, etc.? Consider if this is a project you would like to pursue. If so, go for it!

Journal Prompt: Visualization

You may find that enjoyable and calming images are most helpful to you as mental images. Mental images can be held in time or they can evolve as you wish. The benefits of allowing time daily to meditate can be felt immediately and can result in lasting, healthful outcomes.

Visualization was an active approach I took to combat the stress and anxiety of attempting another pregnancy. I visualized my body functioning effectively to carry nourishment to my baby. I pictured the placenta and the developing sack protecting my baby. I then visualized my baby moving and growing in the womb. I pictured arms and legs moving. I studied the tiny fingers and toes. I pictured the heart pumping and paused to watch the quick fluttering movements of a healthy heart. I studied these images in my mind and they became as calming for me as studying a sleeping child. Focusing on these images at night before I went to sleep enabled me to avoid the anxiety at the thought of losing another baby.

I realized that if stress and negative thinking could effect my body in a negative way, then I wanted to focus my attention and energy on positive outcomes. Taking care of myself by nurturing my mind and my body became for me, a form of mothering my baby. Focusing on healthy food choices, exercise, and relaxation, were important for my health and the health of my baby. I attempted to give my baby, even in the earliest stages, the best of what I had to give. If I lost my baby, I would have the peace of knowing that some outcomes are beyond my control; but where I might have a positive influence, I contributed to my baby's well-being to the best of my ability.

Journal Prompt: Evaluating Personal Needs

Careful evaluation of personal needs can be helpful in easing stresses and allowing you to refocus your energy.

It may be useful to make a list of needs and ways to satisfy them, even if fulfillment seems impossible at this time...(You may find it helpful to share parts of this list with those who would like to help but are unsure of what you may need.)

Part VI

Acceptance
and Other
Observations
Along the Fence
Between
Life and Death

Journal Entry: Acceptance

The loss of a baby due to miscarriage can leave a woman in a vulnerable emotional state. Many find it difficult to recognize the loss, or put another way, to respect the life that was once there. I was told in many different ways I had no right to the emotions I was expressing. There were those who saw no reason for me to even pause to recognize my loss. They questioned my loss as well as my right to grieve. The hurt and the loss are real and must be recognized, embraced, and shared, for healing to begin. I had to learn to accept the pain, the fear, the anger, the frustration, the emptiness, that followed each loss and disappointment. The emotions were a real part of me, with valid reasons for being. The reasons being mine alone. There has been a bond each time I have become pregnant that has been a source of anticipation and joy with each healthy pregnancy. This bond has also been the reason for the pain of each loss.

Women's issues are often dismissed as irrational emotional responses, a result of some trivial or even imagined problem. To the contrary, the roots are often of a deeply rational and spiritual origin. At one point, I expressed the need to have a doctor who cared for the whole person rather than one who maintained an impersonal relationship where the physical condition is the only aspect taken into consideration for treatment. I was fortunate to have a doctor who maintained a nurturing manner. Such a relationship required patience and respect from him. The trust I placed in my doctor was a result of his caring acceptance of me. Looking back, I see that type of relationship was essential in helping not only me but also my family through an extremely trying and painful period. My doctor opened avenues of counseling for the emotional needs that were as necessary to healing as any prescription for a physical ailment. The counseling I received encouraged me to honor my deepest feelings. The experience was referred to often by my counselor as my "spiritual journey."

I have completed an incredible yet exhausting journey. One that has led me down a path of personal discovery, an experience that was as frightening as it was enlightening. One does not always know what will trigger the need for serious self-examination, whether it be the loss of someone you love, a serious illness, the loss of a career opportunity, divorce, etc. Although the experiences are different, if the impact on the individual is strong, the emotional responses are often similar. My experiences with miscarriage and the struggle that followed in trying to have a family resulted in a depression so deep, I did not know if I had the ability to overcome. I still look back on my past and experience an array of emotions. The tears are still fresh, the pain is still a real ache and not just a memory.

I have learned from my experience that I can accept miscarriage, but only on my terms. Those terms being the understanding that I have carried a life that existed for a short time before being taken away. That the life is valuable in and of itself but also to me, as it is my baby in its beginning. And that the grief and sorrow that follows are my own and should not be questioned for the purpose of denying my right to embrace the emotions as fully as I would have embraced my child, had we been given more time together.

As I sit down to write in my journal again, it occurs to me that I am writing from a new perspective. If there is one valuable lesson I have learned in looking into the past, it is to be kind and true to myself. Being true to myself meant gently nurturing my heart, allowing it time to heal. Being true to myself meant listening to my heart to fully appreciate the gift of my babies. It was essential for me to honestly and openly grieve the loss of them. They have left behind a legacy of love as a gift to my family and me. My journal writings are proof of that legacy. The words still move me and affirm that God did not abandon me.

There have been many memories created during the time it has taken me to have my children. Some were written in my journal, others have been pushed aside. My journal has become a necessary vehicle that allows me to revisit those children I lost. At first, I was afraid to go back there. Since I am still vulnerable to the emotions that accompany the memories, I found myself back in that place where the sadness can be all-encompassing. There are times when I allow the memories to come flooding back because I know now, I do not want them to be lost. The babies I briefly carried entered this world through me and profoundly moved me. In return, I could not move on without embracing the loss of them. The obstacles and experiences in the process have left an indelible imprint on me that will have its influence for the rest of my life. The contours of my inner form have been painfully forged in the process. I am convinced this form will continue to take shape and serve to guide me if I have the courage to nurture the presence within, as lovingly and painstakingly as I nurture my children. Along with the birth of my children, I have conceived a truer sense of myself. I believe in part, I have discovered the deeper meaning of Joseph Campbell's statement: "Follow your bliss, go where body and soul want to go. When you follow your bliss, you come to bliss."

E.B.

I struggle to unravel the inconsistencies of miscarriage and grief and my intense need to understand. But as I struggle, I learn and grow. If I take the opportunity to examine my experiences, my efforts are rewarded. I become better acquainted with myself and my God.

Journal Entry: The Windsock

When I imagine all there is to know, I imagine something as elusive as the wind. Complete knowledge, full knowledge, shares many of the same characteristics as the wind. Knowledge and the wind are sublime in their power. Sublime, meaning awe inspiring and supremely moving. Knowledge misused or captured before the individual is ready to hold it can be damaging to the individual. To hold it can be as destructive as the harshest storm, laying waste to all sense of order.

Imagine a windsock, it skims a portion of the passing wind. The wind seems alive and reactive, capable of eventually wearing a shredded hole in the tapered end of the sock. The wind escapes to continue on its pass. Whatever moves the wind will not be held fast. The wind will seep through any container. But we can observe the wind's movements and judge the direction and velocity by hanging out the sock to define it somewhat.

Thoughts and knowledge can be captured in the same way as the wind, but true understanding can be as elusive. My mind is the windsock and I attempt to skim thoughts from the massive pool of knowledge, that is the wind. I attempt to control the direction and flow of those thoughts to enable me to grasp some meaning before they pass to return to their source. Thoughts can be as powerful and dangerously sublime as the wind or as trivial as the slightest breeze that brushes my cheek on an achingly hot day. A hint of a breeze is enough to pique my longing for relief from the heat of day. The dim breeze leaves me wondering if I actually experienced the wind or just felt my own breath. Either way, the brief coolness on my cheek reminds me of the potential of the wind to move through me: entering through the weave of fabric that is my clothes, cooling my body, reviving me, allowing me to breathe freely, dissipating the heat that weighs on me, pinning me down, immobilized.

Trivial thoughts frustrate me as much as a slip of the wind on a hot day. I crave something more substantial, something I can feel a part of, moved by. But in my longing, I am profoundly aware of the intensity and power of something that could crumple me in my fragile state. I do not possess the deepened roots that would lend me the ability to bend and sway without being completely overwhelmed. Knowing this, I continue to skim what I can from the source, hoping to one day have the knowledge or substance to be invited into the depths. There is a presence within those depths. I believe it is this presence, whom those who seek immortality or speak of eternity, wish to meet.

E.B.

Journal Prompt: Stream of Consciousness

Stream of consciousness, refers to the "stream" of ideas that "pop" into your head at any given moment. They are often disjointed fragments or initial observations. These inlets originate from the main body of your thoughts and are potentially the seeds of profound personal insight, like a dream that reveals secrets. This exercise encourages you to follow that stream of consciousness and record those disjointed thoughts for the purpose of examining and expanding them. Stream of consciousness can be a valuable inner resource, to tap into it can be enlightening and personally relevant since the ideas to explore have come directly from you.

To begin, write down whatever thoughts come to mind regardless of whether they seem relevant or related. Later, go back and examine what was written and expand on those ideas that have meaning...

Dear Reader,

This final entry describes a woman going through the process of experiencing life and death. It describes the forced struggle to learn from the disorienting lessons of fear, pain, and grief, which for me, were ingredients of loss. She finds a means of rejecting the negative forces that threaten, to see through the fog, and it is no easy task. Acceptance does not come easily.

In closing, I leave you with some personal thoughts expressing the idea that life is the gathering of experiences from which we come to understand the power of love and our own ability to embrace and nurture it. Death is perhaps a necessary period that in no way destroys the gift of love we have been blessed with in the form of life, but instead is a passage that leads to renewal.

Journal Entry: The Ember

  Claire stood on the borders of death, watching and waiting. For whom, she did not know for certain. She knew only that she would not relinquish her life until He arrived to reclaim the gift. She had carried it for many years, the part of Him He had placed in her. Silently it dwelled deep inside until she discovered the ability to bring it forth. She found the means to stir the black-orange embers and bring them to fruition. As she waited on this final threshold, she looked back on her life. She had no recollection of the time prior to her own birth, except for a conversation she once laid down in poetry. Her poetic soul had pleaded for guidance from Him. He had placed within her life, without her fully understanding why she was entrusted with such a possession. The gift had seen Claire through a chaotic, fascinating, sometimes threatening, always challenging existence, all the while painting images of a place beyond that fed her longing. Claire experienced the longing always, never fully understanding its reason or what it was she longed for, until the day she was terrified by a story she read. Facing an unexpected death, Porter's, "Granny Weatherall," faded into blackness. The only light Granny saw was from her shrinking bedroom, a small and distant speck. Disillusioned and alone, immersed in grief and darkness, Granny resigned to accept her empty fate and relinquished her light.

  Reading the story increased Claire's longing. I did not put myself here, she reasoned. I have no recollection of placing myself in this world. I long for the one who put me here and placed the live embers within me. I intend to relinquish the gift to none other than Him. Instincts must guide me, Claire concluded. Instincts she maintained, were waves of inspiration from a distant source. She had learned to employ words to describe the waves and had learned to trust this newest sense. Through imagery she had walked along ledges with her eyes closed. This means she had employed to become proficient in exercising her ability, "to know." Unconsciously she had been doing it for years. When someone asked if she believed in God, she knew He existed, even as a small child, she knew.

The voice of reason broke into her thoughts at that moment and taunted, "How will you know Him to relinquish the gift?" She replied, "I will give it to no one but Him." The voice further taunted, "What if you are fooled?" She replied, "I will give it to no one but Him." The voice again pressed, "How will you know?" She replied, "I will give it to no one but Him." Some things do not require an explanation she thought, some things you will just know. She knew she would find Him. She waited.

Off in the distance, Claire noticed movement. Walking to meet it, Claire was surrounded by motion discernible only as wisping shadows, interchanging. Motion with voice called to her as it pushed and pulled her. Like the wind, it wound around her, attempting to become a part of her. Matching the rhythm of her breathing and then the increasing tempo of her racing heart, the entity coaxed then raged at her to join the danse macabre. Swept up in dizzying motion, her mind in a whirl, the increasing pull of the vortex threatened to drain her of all coherency. Thoughts fled, stripped away like flimsy paper sheets in a storm. Struggling to interpret her surroundings, Claire watched panicked doves take flight. Straining to focus her energy on widening the vortex, Claire managed to reclaim some sense of balance. Vaguely aware of her ability to do so, she repelled the force. It would not be allowed to flow through her and rob her of the embers. To Claire's relief, during the movement's gradual decline, waves of coherent doves returned to roost.

With movement's departure, Claire was blanketed by fatigue. But the weight of fatigue was swept away by the instinctual forewarning to prey in the predator's midst. Alerted to the predatory advance, Claire grew aware of the invasive entry as an ache in her extremities that coiled inward with a possessive deliberateness. She sensed the border of her being, chilled along the edges, becoming more frigid as she looked inward. Tracing it's icy trail, she cringed as the sensation grew painful in its ability to pressure her. Powerfully thrusting with decisive contractions, the predator stridently demanded her release. Claire recognized her own ability to preserve the ember and the ember in turn provided the contrasting warmth that strengthened her resolve. She labored to shelter the gift, determined not give in to the sensation. It was not Him, although it possessed tremendous strength. Sensing her resolve, the predator abruptly released her, leaving the ember in her possession.

Voices within her head began to speak to her, first reassuringly, praising her resolve. Growing more persuasive, the voices sang out that her task was complete and she had won. She felt a surge of excitement until she realized she was not here to "win." This was not a game with a prize, some polished apple to bite into freely. This place of infinite happiness did not end her search. Unending happiness was not what she longed for. He was not here among the songs of joy and praise. Claire turned away from the sounds of rejoicing and the ember flared. She felt its intensity in the warmth seeping through her to her fingertips. Her breath caught in her throat in anticipation. She moved toward Him, a solitary figure in the distance. The closer she moved, the higher the ember flared. It was burning now without a flicker, an intense and steady flame.

He turned to her and spoke, "How do you know me?" I carry you within me, she replied, and it is burning me. The ember is blazing and I am no longer able to sustain it. It will consume me unless you accept its return and me along with it. She marveled at His quiet countenance. Possessed of power, His form was ever changing, revealing a childlike air then that of an old man, bent but solid, now that of a young boy, playful and free. Emotions explosively spliced each ephemeral silhouette, igniting like sparks from sizzling beads of sap on a burning log. She felt the stirring as the emotions engaged her. Joyful yet painful, with a weightiness of water filling her lungs, the emotions overpowered her until she had no strength of her own. Transfixed, she knew the time had come to choose. Be consumed in the flames by refusing to relinquish the ember or release the gift and know the power of eternity.

She knew His voice, He spoke to her softly she thought but realized she could no longer hear. Voice without sound, He moved her deeply telling her it was time to relinquish the gift. A sudden burst of anger stabbed her; she fought back not wanting to give up what she possessed. She fought like a mother protecting her babe. Calmly he waited, accepting her angry blows. He would not take what was now hers, she sensed it. She realized too, it was not a gift she could easily relinquish. Sorrow engulfed her. She sobbed, intensely aching from within. She did not know then if the agonizing pain was the result of her own grief or if it was from the ember longing as a child to return to his father and not being allowed to go. Father and Son waited for her to decide. She thanked Him again for His gift but cursed Him loudly. The words flowed freely as did the anger and sorrow. The agony fed her anger as she formed the words aimed at Him and forcefully delivered to Him. She showed Him her life through word painted images. She relived the moments, piece by faded piece they unfolded: emotions and memories, talents and knowledge revealed themselves, pain and anguish seeped from hurt-filled foolishness, questions were recalled that had left her immobile with fear. She related it all to Him, her life's events, mostly ordinary, many with little attached, for these she felt ashamed. She realized, throughout her lifetime the ember had burned within, sharing with her the joys, the mundane, and the agonizing sorrow. She recognized His presence in the ember, filling her unconditionally. She learned in the moment that she had not revealed anything to Him that He had not already seen, heard, experienced. She wept.

For an instant she thought she controlled Him. She knew she had in her possession a part of Him. Through a lifetime, she had fostered this essence and now wanted to claim it as her own. How could she give up such a prize, it was life itself? Without it she would wither, she knew that. She was form without life. He was life without form and yet He exuded all things.

She imagined herself cradling the ember like an infant. The image of the Madonna flashed before her. She felt stabs of jealousy and embarrassment. He showed no signs of anger or reproof at her presumption. She was grateful. But the emotion remained and she realized she identified with the Madonna at this moment, being asked to carry a sacred gift and later expected to release it once love had been ingrained. She perceived the ember as her son. It was a true love, the truest she could know. Looking into her son's eyes, she perceived love's purity. Love formed the pristine droplets that fed cool running water to her parched and yearning soul. She recognized her son's love for her but realized his longing. Was it his all along? She thought it was herself longing for another place while she endured the day to day existence, distant from the present.

Love is power, she thought. It binds me to you my son, and I am devoted without regret to watching over you. No one shall hurt you without also hurting me. No one shall touch you without also touching me. With these words the flame leapt. She felt its warmth enveloping her, consuming her. She knew it was time. He had waited patiently. He had given her all she had needed to find this love in the world, a love that is complete, nourishing, and all-consuming. Her maternal like feelings would not allow her to prevent the ember from rejoining its source. She would not rob Him of His Son, her son. She would gladly wither and die than condemn her son to eternal longing. She relinquished the flame and felt herself emptied. Vacated she was no more than a transparent lining, fragile as an onion skin.

She watched the reunion, determined to see it to completion. The reunion brought energy together, power with power, light with light. The resulting blaze was blindingly white. Having seen what she had come for, her loss of sight brought no regrets. The rejoining complete, she prepared for her own end, for the cold bleak finality of her existence without Him, without life. Blinded and withered, she was ready.

Warm and binding They filled her, possessed her, moved her beyond life as she had known it. Pure and true, Their words rang out like a child's song and a lover's serenade. "No one shall touch Me without also touching You." She understood. Love shared with Him and nurtured from within is eternal.

E.B.

Journal Prompt: Record Your Thoughts

Pause for reflection, you may wish to record your thoughts.

Works Cited

Cousineau, Phil, and Brown, Stuart L. eds. *The Hero's Journey Joseph Campbell On His Life And Work.* San Francisco: Harper & Row, 1990.

Dr. Seuss. *Did I Ever Tell You How Lucky You Are?* New York: Random House, 1973. 13.

Leeming, David Adams. *Mythology The Voyage Of The Hero.* Third Edition. New York: Oxford, 1998. 44, 101, 157, 194, 217, 231.

Lewis, C.S. *The Chronicles Of Narnia-The Last Battle.* Vol. 7. New York: Scholastic, 1984. 167-170.

Morris, William., ed. *The American Heritage Dictionary Of The English Language.* New College Edition. Boston: Houghton Mifflin. 1979.

Nilsson, Lennart. *A Child Is Born.* Completely Revised Edition. New York: Dell, 1986.

Porter, Katherine Anne. "The Jilting Of Granny Weatherall." Kennedy, X. J. Gioia Dana. *Literature An Introduction to Fiction, Poetry, and Drama.* 7th ed. New York: Longman, 1999. 70.

"Sacrifice And Bliss." *Joseph Campbell And The Power Of Myth With Bill Moyers* 6 vols. Videorecording. New York: Mystic Fire Video, 1988.

Singer, June. *boundaries of the SOUL...the practice of JUNG'S psychology.* Revised and updated. New York: Doubleday, 1994. 215.

"The Legacy of Loss," *Parenting,* May 1990. p. 76.

Suggestions for Additional Reading

A Silent Sorrow: Pregnancy Loss: Guidance and Support for You and Your Family. Ingrid Kohn. Perry Lynn Moffitt. Dell Publishing. 1992.

A Time To Grieve Meditation for Healing After the Death of a Loved One. Carol Staudacher. Harper. 1994.

Companion Through the Darkness Inner Dialogues on Grief. Stephanie Ericsson. Harper Perennial. 1993.

Empty Arms Coping After Miscarriage, Stillbirth and Infant Death. Sherokee Ilse. Wintergreen Press. 1990.

Empty Cradle, Broken Heart: Surviving the Death of Your Baby. Deborah L. Davis. Fulcrum Publishing. 1991.

Grieving the Child I Never Knew. Kathe Wannenberg. Zondewan Publishing House. 2001.

Miscarriage A Shattered Dream. Sherokee Ilse. Linda Hammer Burns. Wintergreen Press. 1989.

Miscarriage Women's Experiences and Needs. Christine Moulder. Routledge. 2001.

Miscarriage Women Sharing From The Heart. Marie Allen, PhD. Shelly Marks, MS. John Wiley & Sons Inc. 1993.

Our Stories of Miscarriage: Healing With Words. Rachel Faldet. Karen Fitton. Fairview Press. 1997.

Preventing Miscarriage The Good News. Jonathan Scher, M.D. Carol Dix. Harper Perennial. 1991.

When A Baby Dies: A Handbook for Healing and Helping. Rana K. Limbo. Sara Rich Wheeler. Resolve Through Sharing. 1986.

When Bad Things Happen to Good People. Harold S. Kushner. Quill. 2001.

National Support Networks and Services

Bereavement Services/RTS
Gundersen Lutheran Medical Center
1910 South Avenue
LaCrosse, WI 54601
800-362-9567, Ext. 4747
608-791-6747
(Educational materials for bereaved
parents and health care professionals)
e-mail: bereavs@lhl.gundluth.org

Compassion Book Service
477 Hannah Branch Road
Burnsville, NC 28714
704-675-9670
(Books on death, dying, comfort and
hope. This organization is the mail
order division of Rainbow Connection.)

Pregnancy & Infant Loss Center
1421 E. Wayzata Blvd., Ste 30
Wayzata, MN 55391
612-473-9372

SHARE Pregnancy & Infant Loss
Support, Inc.
National SHARE Office
St. Joseph Health Center
300 First Capitol Drive
St. Charles, MO 63301
800-821-6819 or 314-947-6164
http://www.NationalSHAREoffice.com

National Directory of Bereavement
Support Groups and Services
ADM Publishing
PO Box 751155
Forest Hills, NY 11375-8755
718-657-1277
(National and local resources on all types
of bereavement)

Centering Corporation
1532 North Saddle Creek Road
Omaha, NE 68104
402-553-1200
(Catalog available that offers caring
resources in books and pamphlets)

A Place to Remember
deRuyter-Nelson Publications, Inc.
1865 University Avenue, Ste. 110
St. Paul, MN 55104
612-645-7045
(Offers support materials and
resources for those who have
experienced the loss of a baby.)

Wintergreen Press
3630 Eileen St.
Maple Plain, MN 55359
Phone/Fax 952-476-1303

The Rainbow Connection
477 Hannah Branch Road
Burnsville, NC 28714
704-675-5909
(Networking organization offering
publications, training, retreats, and
support to help people grow through
change.)